Today, I have the honor to speak of a woman who not only allowed her life to be changed but also changed my life.

When I first met her, she captivated me with her presence and beauty. I instantly knew she was special. Her mission in life is to prevail against grave and dire obstacles, not only for herself but also to help others do the same.

Over time, I drew myself closer to understand who she was and what she stood for. From the beginning of her life until this moment, she is a living testimony of who God is and the love that He has for us. At one point, she *was* living in hell, but she still saw the hand of God move on her behalf.

As my beautiful wife would say, "if He could do for me… He could do for you…"

Through her life, you might ask, where was God in all her mess? Read this book, and you will get your answer.

In the book of Philippians, Chapter 4 verse 8 ESV, it reads:

"Finally, brothers, whatever is true, whatever is honorable, whatever is just, whatever is pure, whatever is lovely, whatever is commendable, if there is any excellence, if there is anything worthy of praise, think about these things."

When I think of my wife, Dr. Maribel López, I can only give THANKS to my Heavenly Father for blessing me with such a great woman in my life.

-Michael A. Hernandez

My name is Erik Delgado, and I am the eldest son of Maribel López. My mother is the strongest woman I know. Every struggle she went through to get her to where she is today, coming to the United States from Puerto Rico, from having her firstborn at sixteen to earning a Doctoral degree, is nothing short of remarkable.

She always kept her faith, and whenever she would stray away, she still found her way back to stay on course. My mother always pushed through, never gave up, and always made sure her children were cared for. She went to school full time while running a licensed home childcare. It was not easy, but she never gave up. I am proud to call her my mother.

-Erik Delgado

I am delighted to contribute to this foreword, not only because Maribel López is my mother, but also because I believe in her work. She loves writing and genuinely loves her students.

Maribel López, at the core, is an educator and a teacher. I believe her book will enrich your life to the fullest because it will be as if she is there sharing with you, one on one. My mother is an encouraging person. She encouraged me to go to school, graduate college, and follow my dreams.

I graduated from Northeastern Illinois University, and I followed in my mother's footsteps, and now I am a teacher at a Jr. High school. I stay true to my artistic roots and do freelance photography. These are all things she encouraged me to do, and I know reading this book will encourage many to do the same.

-Jose F. Navarrete

I've had the privilege of knowing the behind-the-scenes life of Dr. Maribel López. The one who loves to work from bed and prefers to stay home. She easily drinks three cups of coffee a day, not because she needs it, but because she loves the taste.

I have watched my mom overcome some disheartening things. I have witnessed her grow into this powerful woman, and I am still learning more about her every day. Without a doubt, I know if you read this book, you will not only get to know my mom on a deeper level, but you will find the strength to keep going in Christ Jesus.

-Clarybelle Navarrete – Camacho

My mom is a walking quote and is full of motivation. Growing up, she would tell my siblings and me, "*follow your dreams, never give up, and if you want it, go for it.*" My mom learned this throughout her years because of everything she has endured.

She is a great role model and inspiration to her children and anyone she encounters. As an adult, I enjoy watching her still conquer her dreams and write her book, which she mentioned wanting to do this for as long as I can remember.

If you are a person who wants to learn how someone overcame obstacles and persevered, despite their circumstances, then this is the book for you. You will be inspired to keep pushing through.

-Suzzane Navarrete

God's Not Mad at You

In fact, He loves you

Dr. Maribel López

God's Not Mad at You
In fact, He loves you

Copyright © 2021 Dr. Maribel López

All Rights Reserved.

No part of this book may be reproduced or transmitted in any form or by any means, electronically or mechanically, including photocopying or recording without prior written consent by the author or the publisher of record.

The information contained in this book is based on the life experiences and opinions perceived and expressed by the author.

Published, distributed, and printed in the United States of America by Rose Gold Publishing, LLC.

Book cover photo credit: Jose F. Navarrete, pikaz_photos

ISBN: 978-1-952070-23-5

www.RoseGoldPublishingLLC.com

Copyright © 2021 Dr. Maribel López
All Rights Reserved.

"Scripture quotations taken from the Amplified® Bible (AMP), Copyright © 2015 by The Lockman Foundation.
Used by permission. www.lockman.org"

"Scripture quotations taken from the Amplified® Bible (AMPC), Copyright © 1954, 1958, 1962, 1964, 1965, 1987 by The Lockman Foundation
Used by permission. www.lockman.org"

The Holy Bible, English Standard Version® (ESV®) Copyright © 2001 by Crossway, a publishing ministry of Good News Publishers.
All rights reserved. ESV Text Edition: 2016

Scripture quotations taken from The Holy Bible, New International Version® NIV® Copyright © 1973 1978 1984 2011 by Biblica, Inc. ™
Used by permission. All rights reserved worldwide.

Dedication

With a grateful heart, I dedicate this book to my children, my grandchildren, and their children.

To all who suffer in silence, this book is also for you.

For the ones who feel "I do not have a voice," let me help you.

I am your voice, and you are not alone, you do matter, you do not need to suffer in silence, it was not your fault, you are not condemned, you too can be unleashed, delivered, and saved by the power of our Almighty God through Jesus Christ who died for you, and me at the cross.

Jesus loves you! And I do too!

Acknowledgments

I feel like the most loved woman on this earth! God loves me so much that he has surrounded me with the most amazing, courageous, and encouraging people.

This healing journey has not been easy, and I cannot imagine doing this without my gift from God, my husband, Michael.

Michael, God, brought you to my life precisely at the right time. You are my forever love. I am grateful for the love and support you have given me throughout the most challenging times. You bring love, assurance, and laughter to my life. But most importantly, you bring God every day into my life. I love you.

I want to acknowledge my children, who lived with me through most of my journey and endured pain and heartache. My son Erik, whom I had at the age of sixteen; we grew up together. You have been with me and seen things no child should have experienced. Thank you for forgiving me and loving me unconditionally. You make me so proud to be your mother. You have shown me the meaning of strength. Thank you for standing by my side when I did not do the same for you. I love you.

Jose, you bring me so much joy and love. Tenacity is our middle name, we have never given up on each other, and our love has grown stronger every day. Thank you for being who you are, raw and real. You keep me honest. You challenged me in ways many should be challenged. You love me and care for me in a way a child can only love his mother. Thank you for forgiving me and thank you for being you. I love you.

Clarybelle, my dearest princess; you made me a queen the day you were born. You inspire me and bring me hope and joy. Every time I see you, I see God's beauty, his marvelous works, and God's power of love and redemption. You saved me from me. You brought me into the light and made me realize that I needed to change my life, a task that in the "normal" world belongs to a mother, not the daughter. Together we have challenged the status quo and have challenged all statistics around what a mother and daughter relationship should be. GOD had mercy on me when He gave me YOU. I love you.

Suzzane, our Suzzy; you are my sunshine, my angel from above. I felt the kiss of God when you came into my life. I felt his protection and provision when He brought you to us. You shine my world! Thank you for holding me accountable and not letting me lie to myself about everything being ok when things were clearly *NOT OK*. Thank you for your love and admiration. You inspire me to be the best version of myself. I love you.

To the WISE and BRAVE women in my life, my BFF's and my "Badass Mastermind" sisters, we have shed some blood tears. We held each other up when the other was down and we never let each other fall.

Raquel Toledo, a sister, a friend, with a loving touch, you carry out God's mission and help women like me realize their actual value. Also, I want to thank you for introducing me to Ofelia Perez.

Ofelia Perez, thank you so much for sharing your wisdom with me.

And finally, thank you to all, who in one way or another held me, loved me, guided me, and helped me realize what a precious life I have and how loved I truly am.

Thank you to my family, my friends, and Restored Ministry for all your love and support and believing in me.

Thank you, Dolly Cortes, my Publisher, for all your love, support, guidance and coaching through my writing process. Your integrity and passion for helping others heal through writing is admirable.

The acknowledgments are innumerable. Throughout the years, God has placed individuals along the way to guide and inspire me.

I am ready to share my journey. Are you ready?

Table of Contents

Introduction	1
1. Is There A God?	4
2. He Hurt Me	7
3. Nobody Knew	13
4. We Are More Than Conquerors	15
5. What Are You Looking At?	17
6. Grateful	20
7. Hope is Not Lost	25
8. I Am Who God Says I Am!	28
9. The Fear That Saved Me	30
10. My Gift from God	33
11. My Inspiration	36
12. Trusting Was Not Easy	38
13. Becoming My True Self	41
14. Trust the Process	43

15. God's Got You!	46
16. Do Not Let Anyone Steal Your Joy	48
17. Was a Hot Mess!	50
18. Eternally Grateful Ministry	54
19. Stay Focused…Press On	58
20. Celebrate Your Life	62
21. The Perfect Daughter	64
22. What is God's Will for You?	66
23. Standing in His Love	69
24. Whole, Healthy and Complete	71
25. Prepare for the Battle	74
26. It's All Part of the Process	76
27. Chase Your Dreams	78
28. Do Not Give Your Power Away	80
29. God is Not Mad at You!	86

30. Spring Cleaning, Lessons Learned	88
31. Live the Life God Intended for You	91
32. I Forgive You	95
33. God Loves You, and I Do Too!	98
Reflections	**103**

"For I know the plans I have for you," declares the LORD, "plans to prosper you and not to harm you, plans to give you hope and a future."

Jeremiah 29:11(NIV)

Introduction

Writing my story has been one of the most challenging things I have ever had to do.

Childhood trauma has long term ramifications that plague your very essence. For many years, I lived in shame and doubtfulness, apologizing for being myself because I did not know who I was. The image of "Maribel" was shattered by feelings of being "unloved, unwanted, and unworthy" *lies* the enemy wanted me to believe.

I want to encourage you to write your story, as there is power in writing it. But most importantly so you can start your healing. Notice I did not say publish your story. I said write, but if you do decide to publish, know that you can be helping many people who sometimes feel alone or think to themselves, "this only happens to me." I cannot emphasize the countless times people have come to me after I shared my life story (mostly women) and say, "thank you" or "this happened to me." One of the things some women say that gets to me is, "when you were speaking, I thought you were talking about me," or "that is my life." Hearing those words, is liberating for me in many ways. For the longest, I thought I was the only one going through it all. I was in silence for so many years.

When I was younger, I kept quiet *because of fear*; I kept silent when I got older *because of shame.* Enough is enough! I need to share what the LORD has done in my life because I know many people are suffering when they do not need to. Yes, bad things happened, but it does not have to define you. I want you to know that the enemy wants to keep you quiet, feeling down, depressed, and angry. If he accomplishes this, he has taken your blessings, and most importantly, your peace.

The Lord has been calling me for as long as I can remember, and today, I know why. People live in bondages that can be broken, with lies that can be dismantled. I lived in fear about sharing my story, and every time I started, I could not finish. Through countless therapy sessions, I have taken medications, and all the while, God has been with me through my healing process, always. What held me back was distrust. Sometimes, I have felt like the people of Israel, wondering in the wilderness for 40 years (Joshua 5:6 NIV). This was me, 40 years in the making. I have not been alone. God, and His angels, have been by my side, guiding the way through it all. My prayer for you is that you find comfort, validation, affirmation, and healing through my life story. To know that you have a Heavenly Father who hears your cries, and He cares. Although sometimes you do not see it, God is working on your behalf. He is by your side, and He has a plan for you, which will make things better.

Thank you for joining me on this path. I pray that as you read my story, you too can find liberation from bondages that hold you down. My prayer is that you find love and freedom, just as I did. And know that God's plan for you is not for harm, but rather to prosper you and give you hope and a future (Jeremiah 29:11 NIV).

My story will take you on a journey of love, redemption, restoration, and freedom.

Eternally grateful,

Dr. Maribel López

Chapter 1
Is There a God?

While growing up and enduring vile abuse at the hands of my uncle, I was feeling horrible, lost, and alone. I would wonder, is there a God? Where is this God, I hear my mom speak about?

Ironically, I felt God was with me during the ordeal. Something I cannot explain, and frankly, still cannot explain today. During that time, God was with me. But I questioned, why is He allowing this to happen to me? I was feeling hopeless and helpless.

I remember the first time I read Jeremiah 29:11 (NIV); it was as if the Lord himself spoke into my ear, and it assured me God was not the one hurting me. If this has happened to you in the past, then you know what I am speaking about. If not, then you must experience God for yourself.

God did not stop my uncle or the others from hurting me, but God helped me through it, and He has never left my side. Therefore, I praise Him! I want to share His love and tell you and the world what He did for me; He can also do for you! Jeremiah 29:11 (NIV) changed my life. It freed me to accept love, and to start trusting God.

As a child I was physically, mentally, and emotionally abused, yet I knew God was with me and He has never left me.

The abuse led me to a life of self-destruction and feeling frustrated. Trusting the Lord was difficult. *How can He say I am going to be alright when things were not alright?* When at times, I just wanted to die.

Today I know that evil exists, but I also know there is a God who is good and all evil will end one day.

Whenever I experience difficult times, I rest assured knowing that it is not God hurting me because the plans He has for me are not for harm.

In this book, I share a letter of forgiveness I wrote to myself, and to say that this was an easy task, falls too short of the fact. The truth is that writing the letter and forgiving myself are two different things. On the one hand, yes, I wrote the letter, but forgiveness has been a journey—a journey, nonetheless, worth taking. I am valuable, loved, and accepted, bought by the precious blood of Jesus. You must understand this. You are who God says you are, not what this world full of evil says. You deserve to live in peace. A peace that surpasses all understanding (Philippians 4:7 ESV). It does not mean we will not go through difficult times. Instead, it means, that through it all, you will have peace, love, and joy; all things God intended for His children to have and enjoy since creation.

YES! There is a God; how else would we (human beings) be able to withstand the enemy's schemes if not by the power we have in Christ. There is a God, and He has been there all along. Would you let Him in your heart? He wants to show you His marvelous love. Would you let Him love you? He wants and desires a relationship with you.

"Among the gods there is none like you, Lord; no deeds can compare with yours. All the nations you have made will come and worship before you, Lord; they will bring glory to your name. For you are great and do marvelous deeds; you alone are God."

Psalm 86:8-10 (NIV)

Chapter 2
He Hurt Me

I was a rambunctious little girl. The energy I have today, I have always had—no wonder no one could imagine anything was wrong with me, including my *mami*. Today, my mom still says I was "tremenda," (this means terrible in Spanish with a positive connotation). Some of my childhood memories include singing and dancing or walking to the store to get my brother, who would often run out to buy candy for one penny. Boy, I miss going to the store to buy something for one penny. We bought gum and other hard candies. Other memories I have involve cooking or burning rice or oatmeal.

I would try to cook for my sisters, but I did not enjoy it. By the way, I still burn the rice. I burn water! I do not like to cook, and I am not ashamed to admit it. This is a joke in my family, and my eldest daughter loves this because it assures her that it is ok for a woman not to cook or love cooking, and it is also ok to burn the food.

I do not recall the exact age when the abuse began, but I remember because we were alone in the house, and I had to cook even though I did not know how. My uncle would take care of us at Abuela's house, and I believed that is where he lived. He also lived with us for a while.

Some of the recollections I have involve me in a room with brown panel walls. I remember my uncle on top of me. On other occasions, he used a dog to hold me down. I cannot recall how old I was, but I know in my soul, my uncle was sexually abusing me since I was a baby. How do I know, you ask? The childhood memories most present in my mind are of my uncle abusing me, hiding me, and telling me not to say anything to anybody, especially my mother. I know he must have groomed me from early on. I feared him, and I believed everything he said. If he said jump, I would ask, how high?

Although my uncle was hurting me, I cannot recall any physical pain while being abused. During the act, I felt Jesus was protecting me. Even though I was physically and sexually abused, my recollections of any pain are non-existent. The pain came later when I realized what occurred to me.

Oprah was the first person I told. Just like you heard, but not like you are thinking. I have not met Oprah in person; however, this is one of those positive things about watching television. While watching the Oprah Winfrey Show one day, she shared that her uncle had sexually abused her. As she explained what happened to her, I knew then what my uncle did to me was wrong. Although, not quite sure, I knew what my uncle was doing was not right because he wanted me to keep it a secret. In my little girl's mind, I felt I was doing the right thing. I thought I was protecting my mom and my sisters.

He would say that no one would believe me, and if I said anything, he would hurt them.

I am sharing my story to shine a light on the things perpetrators say to their victims, like the ones I have mentioned. Share with your children, *"if anyone says these things to you, it is wrong, and you must say something."* I wish I could say that children will come forward, but it is not guaranteed.

Once I saw my mom confront a man who was being accused of molesting a little girl. On another occasion, I saw my mom defending herself from someone who wanted to hurt her physically. And even then, I stood quiet and kept being abused. Pay close attention to the children around you. Have they suddenly changed, are they scared, or seem reluctant to see someone or stay with that person? This was not always the case with me. I loved my uncle; he was my family. Perhaps, I did not say anything because I believed he was not a bad person, and I thought this was "normal" between nieces and uncles. Let me remind you, I was a little girl. This happened during the first eleven years of my life.

Pay attention if your child seems unsettled, sad, or anxious. My suggestion is, *for you to never give up on trying to figure out what may be going on with your children.* Life's daily pressures may cloud our judgment, and therefore we may think that sometimes we are going crazy? Well, I would rather be crazy than have my child be abused.

Learn how to communicate with your children. Do not give up. Keep praying and keep the lines of communication open. Provide a safe place for them to talk to you; this may be your loving arms. Hug them as much as possible, have dinner on the table as many times as possible. On the table is where the best conversations take place. I did not tell anyone until I was in my twenties.

My uncle used fear to keep me quiet, to intimidate me. He would threaten me and say, *"if I said anything, he would kill mom or hurt my sisters."* He would use a dog to keep me from moving or leaving the room, even to stay quiet so that no one knew he had me pinned down in the room. Those who know me well know that this is still a struggle for me. Sometimes if caught unexpectedly while a dog comes my way or it is in a room I am about to enter, I freeze. I was trained not to move in the presence of a dog. I was told he would hurt me if I moved. Perpetrators will use anything they can to carry out their plans. They will groom you, and one thing my uncle would say to me was that I was his favorite niece. As I said, I do not recall when the abuse began. However, most of my childhood memories involve him abusing me.

On another occasion, my uncle decided to bring two other men with him to abuse me. My recollection of this event is minimal. For me, it was like an out of body experience.

For years, I hesitated to share this part of my story because of fear; fear of what people would say or think of me, *as if I am the one to blame for the abuse that was inflicted upon me.* I was afraid to share because I believed the lies instilled in me and could not believe it myself. Why would anyone believe me? How in the world am I still alive? These were some of the questions I asked myself.

I am sharing my life story to help someone who has gone through what I went through know that there is a better life than to live in bondage. The bondage that comes from this horrific abuse is one of guilt, shame, condemnation, fears, anxiety, no self-love, and or acceptance.

At one point, I began eating soap. I did not know why at the time, but after some reflection of my past, I realized that I ate soap to possibly cleanse myself of all the dirt that was placed on me because I felt dirty and unwanted. I thought there was something wrong with me.

If this is you or someone you know, please know that the Lord has saved me. He healed my broken heart and reminds me that I am whole, healthy, and complete every day, and He can do the same for you. We were made for so much more; God had a plan then, and He still does today. When we read Genesis (Chapter 3) in the bible, *"the fall,"* that is all we keep in our minds; we forget God's redemption plan for our lives; Jesus Christ, died and rose again. The story did not end at the Garden of Eden! Hallelujah! The story continues, and there is a fantastic ending. Eternal life!

I am writing this book because I know many people are going through a pain that has a cure. And I am on a mission from God to bring healing to their lives. I was born with a purpose and a mission, and so are you.

"The Spirit of the Lord God is upon me, because the Lord has anointed and commissioned me to bring good news to the humble and afflicted; He has sent me to bind up [the wounds of] the brokenhearted, to proclaim release [from confinement and condemnation] to the [physical and spiritual] captives and freedom to prisoners"

Isaiah 61:1 (AMP)

Chapter 3

Nobody Knew

When my parents divorced, my mother worked very hard to provide for my siblings and me. I am the oldest of six, and I had to help my mom take care of my younger siblings.

Until this day, my loving mother continually seeks to serve God and provide for her children. During difficult times, we always had so much love among us, and although she worked a lot during the week, we had family time and enjoyed ourselves on weekends. We would go to the beach, and on most Sundays, religiously, we ate Kentucky Fried Chicken, *mami's* favorite.

Some weekends, our dad would come and take us to his house to visit our grandmother and his sister. We loved going over because most times we would go to the beach. I think my love for the ocean comes from when I enjoyed playing in the water and spending time with my father.

At school, I remember being distracted. At that time, teachers would discipline you with a ruler if they felt you were not paying attention. This may be unbelievable for some, but even if they were not allowed, they did not care, they would still do it. I never forgot this because when I think back about school and learning, I cannot help but think about how difficult it was for me to pay attention in class because I was being abused. All I could think of was my uncle abusing me.

This experience has impacted how I manage my classroom and how I am as a professor today. I felt sorry for "Mari," the little girl who was scared all the time.

I intentionally stay in the Word of God about not being fearful. I have nothing to fear. However, fear was and is sometimes present in my life, and I am often fighting against this emotion. God is not done with me yet. I am not a little girl anymore, and I can defend myself, and God's angels are by my side. One can dismantle the lies behind the abuse and be transformed by God's love and redemption. I choose to be an active participant in my relationship with God. I pray, read the Word, and maintain myself filled with God's promises for my life. I recommend you meditate on the Word, journal, and talk to God.

"But whose delight is in the law of the Lord, and who meditates on his law, day and night. That person is like a tree planted by streams of water, which yields its fruit in season and whose leaf does not wither — whatever they do prospers."

Psalm 1:2-3 (NIV)

Chapter 4
We are More than Conquerors

What I mostly remember of my life as a teenager is my desire to achieve my dreams. I loved going to school, but it was rough. I went to a high school known for its gangs and violence at the time, the famous Roberto Clemente High School in Chicago. When I mention the high school I attended, people either fear me or feel sorry for me. While walking to school, I remember, it was common for students to fight off the gangbangers from bothering them. I remember being targeted by a gang member who wanted me to be his girlfriend; however, he already had a girlfriend. She knew he wanted to be with me, so she tried to jump me because, according to her, I was flirting with him. He would leave flowers at my doorstep and, on one occasion, gifted me a BIG teddy bear for Valentines' Day. Little did she know that at the time, I was too busy going to school and working to help my mom pay for rent and food. On one occasion she challenged me and wanted to fight me; "meet me at 3 o'clock," she said. After classes were done, I could see the crowd forming up outside; I was so scared. But I said to myself, if I do not go outside, this will never end. Long story short, she did not show up. I know it was God who saved me on this day. I would not be here today if she would have showed up. Back then, girls used to slice "pretty girls" faces with a knife. God saved me once again. The enemy wanted to destroy me, but he cannot destroy me. I belong to an Almighty powerful God.

I am sharing this part of my story because I want you to know that there is an adversary who seeks to steal, destroy, and distract you from your goals. Reflecting on this experience reminds me of the many distractions the enemy uses to deter us from our journey. Today I can see that I was Satan's target since inception (do not be surprised, he wants to destroy humanity).

Human beings believe they are in control of their lives, and to some extent, they are, for God has granted us free will. However, we have a creator, a God who is the Alpha and the Omega. He is the beginning and the end; we do not belong to ourselves, nor do we come from monkeys like some like you to believe. As children of the Lord, we must keep our eyes focused on the Lord and *His* will for our lives. I am sharing this story because I know, like me, you probably are fighting bullies every day, or you wonder whether you are supposed to be here. I am here to tell you, YOU ARE! God has bigger and stronger angels fighting and protecting you. Evil may exist, but it cannot defeat us. We are more than conquerors. We have already won the battle.

"No, in all these things we are more than conquerors through him who loved us."

Romans 8:37 (NIV)

Chapter 5
What are You Looking at?

During my teens and well into my twenties, no one could look at me without me getting in their face. I confronted anyone who would stare at me. I was violent. I was angry all the time, and I carried a baseball bat in my car to confront anyone or to defend myself.

I remember one Christmas season, while looking for a parking spot at a major shopping mall, I saw a car pulling out of its parking spot. As I waited for the driver to move out of the space, another car cut me off and took my spot! I was livid! I came out of my car with my bat in my hand and demanded the driver get out of the car so that I could teach him a lesson.

As I got closer to the car, I realized it was an older man, and he looked at me with fear. I walked away and left him alone. While in the store, he would avoid me, and I did not blame him. I felt terrible. It was then that I said to myself that I would not continue to live like this. I had so much anger inside of me, and I did not know how to handle it. I realized when I was not angry, I was sad. I had many emotions built up inside of me. I felt I was not worthy enough to go to church and or to be in the presence of the Lord because I was an angry person and had lots of not-so-good things on my mind. God made me a fighter. He made me this way, and He did it for a purpose. Yes, the reality is that I was an angry child for obvious reasons.

I was taught to be quiet and not talk about my feelings. When I say God knows what He is doing, believe me, He does. I needed to be a fighter to endure so much abuse. Not only did I endure it, but I witnessed abuse in my life that when I found my voice and my fists, I used them. I reverted to violence because of the anger I had inside of me. The more I got into the Word of God, the more it changed me.

The Word serves as a mirror to our lives; *"Do not merely listen to the word, and so deceive yourselves. Do what it says. Anyone who listens to the word but does not do what it says is like someone who looks at his face in a mirror and, after looking at himself, goes away and immediately forgets what he looks like. But whoever looks intently into the perfect law that gives freedom and continues in it—not forgetting what they have heard but doing it—they will be blessed in what they do"* (James 1:23 NIV).

God made us with those characteristics and with a personality to persevere. He needs us to hone-in on those specific qualities and talents gifted to us to accomplish *His* purpose through our lives. Yes, sometimes some personality traits must change for obvious reasons. Nonetheless, celebrate YOU! He made you just the way you are. And He did it for a purpose and for such a time as this.

I am still a fighter but today I do not jump on anyone that appears to look at me the wrong way. I try to love, just like Jesus did. However, I will not and do not keep quiet if I see injustice. I have learned that God loves me just the way I am. Whatever is not pleasing to Him, He will help me in the refining process, and I know He will do the same for you.

Therefore, if anyone is in Christ [that is, grafted in, joined to Him by faith in Him as Savior], he is a new creature [reborn and renewed by the Holy Spirit]; the old things [the previous moral and spiritual condition] have passed away. Behold, new things have come [because spiritual awakening brings a new life].

2 Corinthians 5:17 (AMP)

Chapter 6
Grateful

My childhood was difficult, and my life has not been easy. Through it all, I learned to be grateful. I am happy to share; I have four healthy adult children, and they are all a miracle.

Although I went through such a terrible ordeal, God showed himself to me in so many ways and at many different life stages. I had all the reasons in the world to be mad at God, but I am not. All the mysteries of this world belong to Him. I rest assured knowing one day He will put an end to all this suffering. What is most interesting to me is that although I was not mad at God, I kept thinking *He* was angry at me. Only humans confuse themselves like this. It is insane!

God's plan for humanity from the beginning was for good. He created men and women in His image to rule over the land. However, God gave men and women free will, to choose to love and to know Him.

Adam and Eve fell into temptation and sinned by disobeying God and his commands. God is a God of His Word, and He does not go back on His promise. His Word assures us, *"for God is not man, that He should lie to us"* (Numbers 23:19 AMP).

I used to question God. I would ask, "why do you allow such pain in the world?" This did not come easy to me, but I learned that *He* is merciful, and *He* is allowing humankind to repent. His promise is of vengeance and judgment. The day will come. He is giving us time to repent of our sins, to turn away from our evil ways. You see, God will not allow us to go through something without Him. He already knows we can handle it. He made us; therefore, He knows what we can endure. He equipped us to withstand all the evil in this world because He made us in His image.

I praise Him, and I sing, because I am eternally grateful to God for all that He has allowed me to experience in my life.

Today I am grateful for my life. There was a time when I did not want to live because the pain was too much to bear. I did not know how to process the pain I was feeling. God helped me by sending angels in the form of men and women who took me under their wings and poured love and wisdom into me to help me become the woman of God that I am today.

I am grateful for the opportunity to share my story and, in doing so, help others overcome shame, doubt, fear, feelings of unworthiness, and condemnation.

I am grateful for the four children he allowed to be born through me because I thought I would never be able to have children due to the extent of the abuse. I am thankful for my grandchildren; they are my world.

I am grateful for the good and the bad times because they have taught me to be the woman I am today.

I am grateful for the husband He has gifted me. One of the lies I believed while growing up was that *ALL* men were bad and that *ALL* men would hurt me. And for the longest time, I lived in fear of men, and I did attract the wrong men in my life.

I am grateful I did not let bitterness and unforgiveness plague my heart. I forgave my uncle and all the men and women who hurt me throughout the years.

I am grateful for the mother and father I have. They love me unconditionally. They did not know what was happening to me because I thought I was responsible for protecting them. They were as much a victim as I was, and although I wanted to blame them, they did not commit the act; they are not to be blamed.

I am grateful for my accomplishments! I am a goal-oriented person. Once I set my mind up to do something, I do it. I am a dreamer. Deep inside, I always knew there was something bigger and better waiting for me. I strive to do good, and I follow my dreams. I also love to help others, and I am an influencer. I love learning and growing.

Whenever there is a conference or workshop, I pray for guidance, and I want everyone I know to go and grow with me. I believe once you stop learning, you stop growing. There is power in knowledge, but I say, there is power only if you use it. I want everyone around me to succeed. We were meant to thrive and to live an abundant life. I want to encourage others to continue to strive to achieve their dreams. My kindergarten graduation teacher loved me because I was always helping the other children. That is still me today. And I love it!

I attended a community college and earned a Certificate in Early childhood education. I later obtained an Associate's degree, then went on to my Bachelor's, Masters', and, ultimately, a Doctoral degree. I share with my students that I attended every graduation ceremony. It is important to acknowledge your accomplishments and hard work. This is also important because I was a mom pursuing a college education, and a titi (auntie). I wanted to share the importance of education with the young ones in my family. *Please pass it on, folks!*

In my twenties, I was a mom of four. I purchased my first home, started my own business, and co-founded a non-profit organization, which today still helps and assists women obtain and maintain their childcare licenses. Also, we focus on the wholeness and well-being of the person. Maslows' Hierarchy of Needs Theory, states that all basic human needs have to be met to reach full potential, which is why we provide additional resources because we want to see the women succeed both professionally and personally. We are proud to be able to empower Latina women in establishing a secure economic status in our communities.

As I reflect on my accomplishments, I thank God for giving me the wisdom to follow my dreams. Here is this little girl whose life was nothing short of a miracle; despite all the turmoil in her head and soul, she followed her dreams. I did not do this alone. I had my faith, God by my side, angels He sent to love on me and guide me, and the love and support of family, friends, and mentors.

In all my accomplishments, I am most proud that I *did not lose hope*. If I would have lost hope, where would I be? Where would my children be?

I am writing my story to bring you HOPE. *Hope that comes from the Lord!*

"But those who wait for the Lord, who expect, look for, and hope in Him, Will gain new strength and renew their power. They will lift their wings [and rise up close to God like eagles [rising toward the sun]. They will run and not become weary, they will walk and not grow tired."

Isaiah 40:31(AMP)

Chapter 7
Hope is Not Lost

The Word of God has filled me with love, hope, and joy. People often ask where I get the energy, and the love I have for others, and my answer is always the same, because of Jesus.

My relationship with God has always been a difficult one. I argue, converse, laugh, cry, and I even vent with the Lord. I encourage you to do the same. Our heavenly Father wants a relationship with us. He does not want a religious, check off a list type of relationship; He wants a genuine connection with His children. God is often to blame for all that goes wrong in the world and our lives. And we often call out to him when we need an intervention. But we do not search for Him in other times, in the good times. I speak for myself and from my personal experiences.

I was searching for answers, and God showed up. He showed up in a mighty way. He changed my life. He transformed my being and made me a new person. How, you ask? It took time and effort.

The Lord will not infringe upon you. He is there if you want to accept him and have a relationship with him. However, He will not force his children to do so. If you are a parent, think about your children and how you treat them. Would you force your child to have a relationship with someone they do not want to have a relationship with? I do not think so. Well, the Word says we are His children. God will not force us to do something we do not want to do. He gave us free will. He is not a man to take back His word. Therefore, we must take the first step and trust Him!

I accepted Jesus in my heart, and then I had to believe Him and believe in Him. One of my favorite bible verses is Mark 11:24 (AMP), *"For this reason, I am telling you, whatever things you ask for in prayer [in accordance with God's will], believe [with confident trust] that you have received them, and they will be given to you."* Some Christians say they are Christians, but they do not fully believe in Him or have doubts. I know. I used to be one of them. We are not perfect, and we will falter, but we cannot stay there. We must not have doubt, like Thomas, the apostle. Thomas doubted Jesus' resurrection. He only believed when he saw; he said, *"Unless I see in His hands the marks of the nails, and put my finger into the nail prints, and put my hand into His side, I will never believe,"* (John 20:24-29 AMP). Wow! How many of us think like Thomas? We need to see, check, and re-check before we believe; even if we saw the miracle for ourselves, we still doubt. In my opinion, this is weak faith; there is no power in that kind of faith. There is power when we believe and act upon it; *"Faith without work is dead"* (James 2:14-26 AMP).

"What good is it, my brothers, and sisters, if someone claims to have faith but has no deeds?

Can such faith save them?"

James 2:14 (NIV)

Chapter 8

I Am Who God Says I Am

I am a passionate woman who loves life. I am a warrior, and a conqueror, just as God says! One of my gifts is connecting with individuals. I am a natural-born leader seeking to better myself every day. I am a daughter of the Almighty King, wife, mother, and a loved grandmother. I am chosen, set apart, a co-creator alongside with God. Persistence and determination are some of my strengths. I am loyal and will fight to the end.

I am also compassionate, kind, and a natural giver. I do not mind giving of myself and my resources if I know it will benefit another soul. We are all connected, and what happens to one happens to all. We are all in this together. Although we did not choose to be born, every day, we need to choose to live. Sometimes, we lose our way, and that is ok. It is ok to NOT have it all together. What is NOT ok, is to not care and not value ourselves as we should.

I lived a life of destruction for many years. I had to ask God for forgiveness, but even more, I had to forgive myself. This is important for everyone to know. God has given us the wisdom to live better lives than the ones we sometimes become complacent to. Complacency is scary to me. Is it a fallacy? Ask yourselves, why are you too comfortable? I want to live the abundant life as mentioned in the Word of God.

The legacy I want to leave my children and grandchildren is me living a life that is pleasing to the Lord and honoring Him by living my life in love, joy, kindness. We only have one life, and I want to live it to the fullest. I want to be true to myself and my beliefs, not lower my standards for anyone. I want to impart forgiveness, love, and kindness because this is what I have learned from the Lord. I want to pass this on. Life is good, and I want to share it with the world! Sometimes the things we live in our lives put a cloud over the promises of God and what He has instore for His children. Live with the expectancy of a better tomorrow. Do your very best today. Let go and let God see what marvelous things He will do in your life.

> *Jesus said to her, "Did I not say to you that if you believe [in Me], you will see the glory of God [the expression of His excellence]?"*
>
> John 11:40 (AMP)

Chapter 9
The Fear that Saved Me

All fear is not bad. Before you mention, "I am contradicting myself," let me explain. The Word of God says, *"the fear of the Lord is the beginning of knowledge (wisdom) but, fools despise wisdom and instruction."* (Proverbs 1:7, KJV). After being alone without a partner for a while, I met someone; we will name him "Allen." He was tall, dark, and handsome, and oh so charming, just a lovely guy with a bad streak. The only thing, he had no job, no car, still in school and living with mama. He loved the Lord and served Him. Oh, but he was at my back and call, he said "I got your back," no one's ever said that to me. That only happened in the movies. The fact of the matter is that *he* became my project.

As I reminisce and wonder what brought us together so close and so fast; I think it was the love of music and our broken hearts. I met him at church; he played my favorite hymn, "How Great is Our God," and come to find out, it was also his favorite. We looked at each other and said; what are we singing? And he started playing my favorite hymn.

The last time I connected with someone through music was my dad when I was five years old. This is why we need to resolve past issues before moving on to new things in life. It is so important. In my case, ALL the red flags were there, but I did not pay attention or did not recognize them because I was too busy "doing" or "rescuing." Shortly after hanging out and meeting his mother, I find out he was battling a drug addiction. He never mentioned this to me.

This relationship forced me to look deeper into my life. How did I attract him into my life? We were both broken, lost, looking for God and love; We were feeding each other's needs. I was obsessed with him, and he was obsessed with me. My friends and family could not understand how or why I was with him. I was blinded by the need to rescue him and fill something in me. After learning of his abuse and also observing him, I knew he was not doing what he needed to do to be on the path to a drug-free life. I decided to end our relationship. It was one of the hardest things I have ever done. Let's not forget I am the oldest of six siblings and the one who helped my mother raised them. I fixed things. I helped anyone who needed help and was successful at it. Not this time. He overdosed; I asked God, "why?" I tried to get him help. I provided him with resources and assisted him in all that I could.

After a short time, I received a phone call from his mother, and she said he was in the hospital on ventilators, with no hope of surviving. Police reports stated it was an overdose. I felt guilty; why did I stop talking to him? Perhaps, if I would have pushed further, this would not have happened. He was already seeing a psychologist and was attending substance abuse classes. No one at this point could have saved him but himself. I sought out therapy for myself because now I was blaming myself.

As I reflect on this experience, I can see that fear saved me. One of my prayers is for guidance. We must take care of ourselves. What good would I have been to him if I would have gone on the same path as him? Fear is seen as negative, which is true when we fear things that genuinely are a fallacy. For example, there is a monster in the closet, or not taking risks, or making changes in your life because you are afraid of the unknown. How is the Lord trying to save you? Have you asked Him for guidance? He is a good father. Ask, and you shall receive. Do you believe?

"The fear of the Lord is the beginning of wisdom, and knowledge of the Holy One is understanding."

Proverbs 9:10 (NIV)

Chapter 10

My Gift from God

After the passing of my friend, I was devasted and fell into depression. What is worse, here I was again, questioning God. Why did I come to this world to suffer? I asked God. I felt defeated and abandoned. And here I was thinking I was done blaming God for everything in my life, and I did it again.

In one way or another, most of the men who had been in my life intentionally or unintentionally hurt me. This was the first time I had established a nice, friendly relationship with a man, who frequently said, "I got your back." And then he died.

I was angry, but more than angry, I was saddened by the whole situation. I prayed to God and questioned him again. At the time, my heart desired to be happily married and settled in my home with my family. And I was alone again, without a partner, without a husband. The dating scene was old, and I was done with it.

I decided to pursue a doctoral program, and I settled for one which suited my needs. I was happy because this program would require all the students to a two-week stay for the next three years, every summer at the George Williams College in Lake Geneva.

When I was younger, I dreamed of going away for college; it was one of my dreams. If I accepted this program, this would become a reality, and I did not know this at the time. But the Lord returned to me what the enemy had taken from me. This place was special to me. My BFF and I have visited this area for the past 20 years. I took it as a sign and said, "yes, this is my program."

As I was driving to Lake Geneva, I went on social media and asked for prayers as I started my new journey. And one person texted me and said, "I pray for traveling mercies, may God protect your going and coming." Maybe in other words, but that is precisely the sentiment. It surprised me. This text came from a man I had met at a mutual friend's recording studio. We said hello and goodbye.

I must be candid with you. You know those Hollywood movies where two individuals' eyes meet, and they stare for a while? Well, without exaggeration, that is exactly what happened with us. Our eyes locked; I thought he was so handsome and so polite. He won me at "hello." Yes, just like the movie, jajaja… As I walked to my car, I dismissed that I had an immediate attraction to this man. And here he was texting me this beautiful prayer. Again, I thought this was nice, but I thought to myself, "I started this doctoral program, and it was not the time to start a romantic relationship."

God is so awesome! You see, His ways are not our ways. When you are a child of the Almighty God, you are genuinely not in control. He has a plan, and He will get it done, with or without you. God can do far more than you can ever imagine (Ephesians 3:20, AMP). I said yes to this relationship, and from the very few first dates, we knew there was something special and we knew God had placed us together. He is my gift from God.

I never knew a man like my husband; respectful and loving. What won me over was the way he treated his mother. I am not sure who said this, but yes, ladies, pay close attention to the guy you are dating and how he treats his mother. One of the two will occur; he will treat you worse or better. Before him, I had never been treated with so much love and care. This man is the epiphany of what the bible says about husbands. *"Husbands love your wives [seek the highest good for her and surround her with a caring, unselfish love], just as Christ also loved the church and gave Himself up for her"* (Ephesians 5:25, AMP).

When I met my husband, I felt the love of God ever so strongly. It was like I received a hug from Heaven, directly from my heavenly Father. God knew that I could not take another disappointment, and He sent me a gift from above. My husband, Michael.

"I remain confident of this: I will see the goodness of the Lord in the land of the living."

Psalm 27:13 (NIV)

Chapter 11

My Inspiration

Experts say that the number one role model in a girl's life is her mother. Regardless if she is deemed a good mother or not. I must say I have the best role model in the world. My mother is my inspiration. From such a young age, my *mami* took care of herself and her brothers. She worked hard. And just like myself, she knew there was something better for her life. The memories I have with my mom are unforgettable.

My mother always looked pretty. She was a fighter, goal-oriented, focused on her dreams, and her FAITH is immeasurable. I have a mother who loves and serves the Lord. She always strived for better, but not only for herself. But for others around her, her children, family, and friends. My mother treasures family, because in her own words, "she did not have one." It was and still is my mother's goal to keep her family together. She does not let us fall. I do not know how she does it! But everyone in our family feels special, loved, and "wellas" favorite. My mother also keeps me going. She does not like me to get sad or discouraged; she starts to pray and activates her faith.

My mother is the image of courage and strength. One thing that has become our family's legacy is our family time. Today, I practice this very same thing I learned while growing up with my mom. It is a beautiful thing. Spend time with your families. Life is too short.

If you have disconnected from your family, try to connect again. Let bygones be bygones, love one another as Christ loves us. If you do not know how to love, ask God for whatever you ask in Jesus' name, believing you will receive, you shall receive, according to His will and purpose (John 14:3 AMP; Romans 8:28 AMP).

We all need some inspiration. Who inspires you? Learn from them. Do not be afraid to ask questions.

I love sharing my endeavors with my mother. Whenever I must make a big decision, I ask my mother, what do you think? She is a wise woman; she lived a long life with trials and tribulations, what she learned in life no school will ever teach. In the end, I make my own decision, but it is always wise to seek counsel.

> *The way of fools seems right to them,*
> *but the wise listen to advice.*

> Proverbs 12:15 (NIV)

Chapter 12

Trusting Was Not Easy

Once our sense of security is tampered with, it is difficult to trust, even God. However, we must understand that God does not ask us to do something that He has not already equipped us to do. We need to ask Him for help and wisdom, and He will graciously give it to us (James 1:5 AMP).

We also need faith; we can ask God for faith (Ephesians 2:8-9 AMP). *"Now faith is the assurance (title deed, confirmation) of things hoped for (divinely guaranteed), and the evidence of things not seen…"* (Hebrews 11:1 AMP). Please know we have a Heavenly Father who cares what happens to His children.

My life was not an easy one. Still, it is not. Those demons still sometimes want to haunt me. I remind myself every day to trust God. I must get into His Word and adopt His ways, not mine. The Word says, *"Trust in the Lord with all your heart, and do not lean on your understanding"* (Proverbs 3:5 ESV). The emphasis is "*with ALL your heart and do not lean on your understanding.*" We fail when we rely on our understanding. We need to go to the source—our creator.

I do not know about you, but I do not understand many things in this world. I have learned to trust in a loving and powerful God. He knows best, and ALL will work for the better of us. Listen, I know it does not always come easy, but it is so important to ask God for guidance, wisdom, and faith. His Word says, *"if we need wisdom, ask, He will graciously give it to us"* (James 1:5 ESV). God's wisdom does not come like you think it should. His guidance is subtle. Are you listening? Is there too much noise in your life? Who do you turn to for guidance? Assurance? Love?

Some of the things I have accomplished in my life have been unbelievable despite the many barriers that existed. I asked God for wisdom and guidance and even though I have not always been obedient, He has been faithful. He has been there when I felt lost and could not think for myself because I stood in His Word. God's Word is clear and powerful.

Some people find it difficult to understand, and this may be because they lack discipline in studying who God is. Do you know your Heavenly Father? How would you get to know Him if you do not study the Word? I ask you to seek counsel, ask pastors, spiritual leaders but more importantly ask God. Buy different versions of the bible and find one that is best suited for your learning style. If you are like me, you would want a print copy. But if finances are a barrier, then use online resources. There are many. And although you must do your research, pray, ask God to guide you, and start searching, your Heavenly Father will see and reward you. I know this due to personal experience. I sought out a relationship with God, and I have it and He continues to guide me. That is the God we serve. A loving God.

Ask, and it will be given to you; seek, and you will find; knock, and it will be opened to you.

Matthew 7:7 (ESV)

Chapter 13
Becoming My True Self

Growing up, I struggled with identity and personality issues. I realize much of my rebellion and discord with God had to do with the "who am I" question. Why was I even born? Why am I supposed to be here? One of the bible verses that helped me on my path to knowing who I am is Psalms 139:13 (ESV), where it reads, *"God created us and knitted us together in our mother's womb."* When this Word came to me, I was in a terrible place in my life. I did not want to live anymore. I did not know what to do with myself or how to raise my children. I was lost. I remember once walking into a church and sitting in the back; I often did this. I did not feel worthy of being in a church. That was a lie the devil wanted me to believe.

I was sitting on the pew with my head down, and someone (whom today I still call an angel) came close to my ear and read this bible verse to me, "For you created my inmost being -you knit me together in my mother's womb," I really cannot explain the feeling, but I will try. I felt as if God himself held me in His arms and told me, "I love you so much, I took the time to knit you together in your mother's womb" even more, I heard him deep in my soul, I chose Marisela to be your mother. AHH!!! Seriously, I cannot explain it better. But

YES! That is precisely how I felt him. After this encounter, I asked my mother for forgiveness because I had treated her with disrespect. I was cold and angry, which I realized later in life had to do with repressed feelings of abandonment and rejection.

After that moment, my life turned around for the better. You see, people talked about this amazing God, that for some time now, I was doubting. I wanted to feel and know the Lord for myself. I wanted to know that I belonged. Something changed in me once I knew I belonged to God and to my *mami*. I knew I was loved. Now, I was on my way to finding myself and reconciliating with mom, dad, and my Heavenly Father. All of which took a very long time.

I hope that after reading this book, you have been able to appreciate how this was done. Perhaps, it will save you years of heartache and sorrow. I am sharing tools that helped me along the way, and it always involved God, prayer, and meditating on His Word.

I did not teach myself to forgive and have faith. This came straight from God. He taught me how to forgive when He forgave me, and He taught me to have faith by gifting me grace every day.

Yet to all who did receive him, to those who believed in his name, He gave the right to become children of God.

John 1:12 (NIV)

Chapter 14
Trust the Process

I say this to my students all the time; "trust the process." Although I know it is difficult to trust a process that comes with so much uncertainty and pain, there is only so much that we can do. The rest belongs to God. I try not to focus on what I cannot do, instead focusing on what I can. For example, while I am writing these lines, we are going through a pandemic. While there is so much, we can and can't do during a time when so many people feel lost and hopeless, we need to focus on the ways in which we can all come together to help each other through this difficult season. I love the assurance of knowing that no matter what happens, God has our back. He is the only one who does, not any circumstances, not the government, not your mom, not your dad, nor your friends. It is only God.

Trusting the process means taking things one step at a time, doing what we can, and helping others along the way. It is doing what needs to be done now, in the present moment, without worrying about tomorrow. It is doing good, even when no one is watching because it is for the greater good and because what happens to one happens to all.

Trusting the process is *trusting* that everything is going to be alright despite_____ (you fill in the blank). Think about all the times you have overcome an obstacle. If you are reading this book, it is because you believe in something greater. It is because you strive to do your very best and want to do better every day. In some ways, you may also be reading this book because you feel some way about God. I am here to tell you to trust the process, and to trust God; it brings a sense of tranquility and peace. Please do your best, and let it take its course. What good does it do for us to worry? I choose not to worry, instead I decide to do what I can and leave the rest to God. Ask yourself; who do you trust? Where is your trust placed? Is it placed in people, things, or finances? I learned early on that we cannot rely solely on people for anything, my full dependency is on the Lord. I know that "things" will not bring me peace. There were many times when I tried to calm my worries with food and other things. It does not work. I have learned that even money comes and goes for it isn't real.

My trust is not in the things I can see. I put my faith where it matters, in the creator, the one who knows it all, the one who will not fail. He has demonstrated this time and time again. He did it for the people of Israel. He did it for Abraham, Isaac, and Jacob. Why would He not do it for us? He will come through powerfully just like His Word says, He goes before us, and behind us, and He will not forsake you. Find comfort and peace in God, a peace that surpasses all understanding (Philippians 4:7 ESV). He did it for me and He will do it for you.

Do not be anxious about anything, but in every situation, by prayer and petition, with thanksgiving, present your requests to God. And the peace of God, which transcends all understanding, will guard your hearts and your minds in Christ Jesus.

Philippians 4:6-7 (ESV)

Chapter 15
God's Got You!

If you have accepted Jesus as your Lord and Savior, you are God's child. You are the child of the Almighty God, the creator, and the maker of the heavens and the earth. The one who gave His only son to die for us so that we may have eternal life (John 3:16 AMP). It only took a minute for me to say, *"Jesus forgive me, come into my heart, I receive you as my Lord and savior,"* but it took me a lifetime to live as a Christian who truly believed it. Deep down in my heart, I always knew there was a God. He was with me when I was being raped, and when I failed to end my life. People adore many different gods. One thing I learned is that we need to know who our God is and what He does. Who is your God?

My God is the Almighty, *"the Alpha and the Omega, the First and the Last, the Beginning and the End"* (Revelations 22:13 NIV). The one who is always right by my side and does not leave me or forsake me (Deuteronomy 31:6 ESV). That is who my God is. How did I get here? I got here through many trials and tribulations. I saw God through the miracles in my life. I still see His blessings in my life every day when I open my eyes. The mere fact that you are reading this tells me you experienced a miracle today. You are breathing and you are alive. Even more, you are striving to grow spiritually and hopefully in your relationship with God. Put all your cares, hopes, and dreams in God's hands for He has got you!

The Word of God says, "*when you seek the Lord, with all your heart, you will find Him*" (Jeremiah 29:13 ESV). He rewards those who seek Him and abide in Him (Hebrews 11:6 ESV). Staying in the Word has provided me with guidance; the Word of God is a lamp unto our feet (Psalms 119:115 ESV). I cannot stress this enough. Whoever shall need wisdom, ask God. When I needed wisdom and guidance in my own life, He upheld His promises as He saved my children and me.

Today we enjoy a life that I never could have imagined. There are going to be problems within everyone's lives, but what's important is knowing that God is with us and if we allow Him, He will guide us through those problems. And God is so far from done on this earth. His Word says that all the earth will know of His glory, Amen!

> *"For the earth will be filled with the knowledge of the glory of the Lord as the waters cover the sea."*
>
> Habakkuk 2:14 (NIV)

Chapter 16

Do Not Let Anyone Steal Your Joy

What happens when you feel sad? It feels like someone took the life out of you. That is precisely what happens when we allow people and circumstances to steal our joy. They suck the life out of us. We feel defeated. The Word of God states that *"the joy of the Lord is our strength"* (Nehemiah 8:10 ESV). When I read this Word, it empowered me. It meant I should not let anything, or anyone take my joy because my strength will be taken as well.

Have you ever felt fatigued? Well, that is what I feel when I let things steal my joy. I feel exhausted, and sometimes when this happens, I wonder what is going on. For example, when I watch the news, sometimes I feel hopeless because of all the negative things that transpire around the world. The important thing here is to be vigilant of the things that affect us and be wise. You can listen without letting things engrave in your hearts and minds. Limit the time you spend watching the news. In the end, put your hope and faith in God's promises, not on things of this world. His Word says, *"Heaven and earth with pass away, but His words will never pass away"* (Matthew 24:35 NIV).

We cannot allow ourselves to stay sad or joyless for too long. However, we can get sad, we can weep, it is good for the soul from time to time. We are humans. I am stressing not to stay there too long; you may fall into a hole much deeper and harder to climb out of. If you feel you need professional help, then seek a good doctor and counselor who can assist you in the process. God is the creator of them as well. He will not lead you astray. The Lord will help you through your journey. You are right where you are supposed to be, let God do the rest. However, He needs you to do your part. Seek Him first and all His things first (Matthew 6:33 NIV).

We need to cling on to the promises of the Lord when times get tough. We need to *"rejoice, pray, and give thanks,"* for it is His will for our lives (1 Thessalonians 5:16-18 ESV). That is one of my favorite verses for it allows me to live abundantly, and in God's presence every day. Every day we can choose to be joyful even through disappointments because every day we can give thanks for His blessings. We must choose to live joyfully, for if we lose our joy, we lose our strength.

Then He said to them, "Go your way. Eat the fat and drink sweet wine and send portions to anyone who has nothing ready, for this day is holy to our Lord. And do not be grieved, for the joy of the Lord is your strength."

Nehemiah 8:10 (ESV)

Chapter 17
I Was a Hot Mess

I was diagnosed with depression, my weight fluctuated, I could not keep a healthy relationship, and I had no established healthy boundaries in my life. I lived dangerously; I went to places I should have never been. I lied when I did not like something or someone. I was angry and unhappy with myself. I just did not have my priorities straight. I hurt people the people I loved, because I was reckless, and I did not know any better.

I hurt my children. In their intentions to follow what they think is right, parents forget they have little ones watching them. They are watching our every move. The way we walk, eat, or drink, especially what we say and who we talk to. If you tend to be a person who thinks, "life sucks," what do you think your children will think? They will think like you and do as you do, not as you say. Although we like to dismiss our elderly quickly, let me tell you, some have lots of wisdom. They've already been down that road. They did what we should not do.

They are warning us. And I digress.

What I am trying to say is that what we do affect those around us. When I started going to church and fell in love with Jesus and His Word, I shared my excitement and Jesus with everyone I encountered. On the road to heaven, I lapsed, and those who were believing alongside me also lapsed. I can only imagine what they thought. "Everything Maribel said was a lie, and now she is doing everything she said God does not want for our lives." I felt scolded like the prophet Ezekiel. He was supposed to maintain watchfulness and bring truth to the people of Israel.

The Lord told him, *"you will surely die, and you do not warn them or speak out to dissuade them from their evil ways to save their life, that wicked person will die for[b] their sin, and I will hold you accountable for their blood"* (Ezekiel 3:18 NIV). I felt as if God was saying the same thing to me.

I sat down with my four children and asked them for forgiveness. I did not offer any explanations, and they did not need them. They needed to know they had a mother who was sorry and that she loved them. Please pay very close attention to what I am saying. When you hurt someone, it does not matter how many reasons (or excuses) you might have (in your mind) to justify your behavior. The truth of the matter is you hurt them. If you have not yet experienced the beautiful gift of forgiveness, I encourage you to try it. Just say that you are sorry because that is all you need to say.

The Word of God is clear on this; it says, *"leave your gift there before the altar and go your way. First be reconciled with your brother, and then come and offer your gift"* (Matthew 5:24 ESV). These gifts are about the offerings and tithing we bring to church to the altar.

For those of you looking for an excuse not to give or bring offerings, well, here you go! You got one! But know this, unforgiveness blocks all the beautiful blessings that come from it, like, healing.

Is there someone in your life you need to forgive? Is there someone in your life you need to apologize to? The Lord is clear here. He is saying before you gift, forgive. Hallelujah! Praise God! I get excited because the Lord is always right! Forgiveness freed me! I needed to forgive those who hurt me, including myself. This is an everyday battle. God forgave me. Therefore, there is no condemnation in my life. Jesus died for our sins.

What I want you to know is that God will transform your life. He will *"bestow on you a crown of beauty instead of ashes"* (Isaiah 61:3 ESV). He will do this by accepting that Jesus died for you on the cross to bring you salvation. By trusting and believing in God, by maintaining a relationship with the Lord through prayer and studying the Word, your life will be changed. The Word *"renews your mind,"* which in turn will change your life (Romans 12:2 ESV). *"And we all, with unveiled face, continually seeing as in a mirror the glory of the Lord, are progressively being transformed into His image from [one degree of] glory to [even more] glory, which comes from the Lord, [who is] the Spirit.* (2 Corinthians 3:18 AMP). If you are like me, you have tried everything else. And still have not reached fulfillment. It is because the only one that can fulfill our very soul is Jesus!

Do not conform to the pattern of this world but be transformed by the renewing of your mind. Then you will be able to test and approve what God's will is—his good, pleasing, and perfect will.

Romans 12:2 (NIV)

Chapter 18
Eternally Grateful Ministry

Eternally Grateful Ministry was born out of gratitude for what the Lord has done in my life. Through this ministry, I share my testimony in hopes of helping individuals, especially women, to free themselves of guilt, shame, and doubt, which does not belong to them. With my husband's help, we self-published a journal titled Eternally Grateful- Eternamente Agradecida (2017). This journal has bible verses that have helped me in my healing process. While journaling, I meditated on the Word. I wrote about what I felt the Lord was saying to me. I also asked God for guidance when I could not make sense of what I was reading. Journaling, for me, is like talking to God.

I am a miracle, and I am here because God saved me. I serve the Lord because I believe in His sacrifice and healing power. While I was leading the music ministry at church, the pastor suggested we record a CD and hold a concert to preach the gospel and fundraise for the church. I was reluctant. As it is custom, I pout, and God speaks. We did the concert, and it was a success. People came, and we received lots of testimonies. One of the many that touched my heart was a woman from Ecuador, who was a self-proclaimed atheist. She stated she never believed in Jesus. She shared how when she was diagnosed with terminal cancer, she sought out help, and was searching for the God people talked about. While searching through the radio stations, she heard the host of the radio program mention, he was playing a song from a Christian singer in Chicago who just released an album. She decided to listen to the song, while she was listening, she said she heard the Lord calling to her. She dropped to her knees and cried out to Him. Today, I am happy to report she was healed. As a result, she accepted Jesus as her Lord and savior, and her whole family is also saved.

I knew once again; God has a plan. I did not know this concert was going to serve as a venue to save so many lives. I began to share my testimony little by little and continued to ask God for guidance and support. While sharing my testimony at different events, women came forward and shared how they, too, had been sexually abused or were survivors of domestic violence. I became burdened with finding words to share with them on how God helped me heal. One night I asked God, Lord, please help me, how have you been healing me? Why am I doing well while others seem stuck or still hurting? I heard God loud and clear, "Show them how I helped you." How did you help me? I asked. He answered, "by journaling, not just writing, but by explicitly writing down the bible verses, meditating on the Word, and recording it in your journal." When I began writing the Word of God, it planted the seeds that gave fruit to what the Lord wanted for my life. The Word of God saved my life.

I journaled, prayed, and asked God to reveal what He wanted me to know about Him and my life. I want to encourage you to do this alone with God. There are a few scriptures where you can read about God's whispers. One of my favorites is when the Lord appeared to Elijah, "After the earthquake came to a fire, but the Lord was not in the fire. And after the fire came to a gentle whisper. When Elijah heard it, he pulled his cloak over his face, went out and stood at the mouth of the cave." Then a voice said to him, *"What are you doing here, Elijah?"* (1 King 19:12-13 NIV). I can almost see the Lord calling on us, but often we are too busy, and there is too much noise in our lives to hear Him. Give it a try, find a quiet place, create a prayer room, and talk to your Heavenly Father, and do not forget to listen.

My heart aches for people who are sad, lost, and depressed. Jesus is the answer. Only God can fill the void in our lives. That is what happened to me. I felt lost, scared, angry, sad, and did not know what to do, and then He saved me. The Word came alive in my life. And here I am, eternally grateful to my Heavenly Father for saving me and for saving my family.

His Word says, *"that my children and my grandchildren will be blessed."* (Deuteronomy 7:9 ESV) I believe it. I decided to talk to God and spend time with Him. I knew of Him and wanted to learn more about Him and what He said He would do. I was intrigued. No wonder I am Dr. López, so inquisitive!

I gave myself a chance—a chance to believe and change my life. I wanted more! I knew we were made for more! I worried about my children. What consequences were they going to suffer because of my actions? One of the things that led me to go deeper with God was my children. They did not ask to come into this world. The Lord entrusted their lives to me, and one day I will have to answer to God. What did I do with my children?

Whether you turn to the right or to the left, your ears will hear a voice behind you, saying, "This is the way; walk in it."

Isaiah 30:21 (NIV)

Chapter 19
Stay Focused…Press On

There are too many distractions that deter us from the essential things in life, but most importantly from God. We were born to do great things. Yet, as we call it, life happens and gives birth to different terrible feelings and lies that keep us down. Your past does not have to define you. So many times, we allow it to define us. I lived with so much doubt and condemnation. I was plagued with guilt, one that did not belong to me, and this is a destructive way to live.

My focus was different; I relied heavily on worldly things and the acceptance of others. Not only did I suffer, but my children suffered even more. I cannot live with guilt, shame, and doubt, and neither should you. When we live this way, we negate what Jesus did at the cross. And we hurt innocent people. Yet, I learned to reflect on past mistakes, learn from them, and move forward. Even the smallest of lessons are crucial to making small changes and moving forward. Stay connected to the cross so that you may not fail. God will not let us fail.

We tend to torture ourselves with the mistakes that we have made, to the point where it feels like the world is over. In reality, mistakes are just part of life. I have made so many mistakes, learned from them, and started fresh all over again.

Please do not ask me how many times I have tried something and began again. This book, for example, is my third time. I have published two other books, "Eternally Grateful Journal," which is how I share how God helped me heal. But in all honesty, I did not share my testimony in full detail because I was not ready. One thing I learned about healing is that it is a process. Do not try to rush the healing wagon. It does not work that way. At least for me. Think about it, when you are dragging a wagon with lots of stuff, it tends to fall. The same thing happens to us. When we try to rush it, we fall, and it feels like we are failing. Sometimes we even start to feel like we are unworthy and rejected by God. That is so far from the truth. God loves us. He created us. Do you think He does not know who you are and when you are going to fail? God knows all things. The Word says he knows *"the very hairs of your head, and they are numbered"* (Luke 12:7 NIV). Ah! That is so awesome!

We serve an AWESOME God!

The second book I published was inspired by my students and for my students. In this book, I share some quotes and life lessons that assisted me along my academic journey. I shared how I got up every day believing I could and ways I pressed on towards my goals. I say "perseverance" is my middle name. No matter what you are going through right now, no matter here you are in the healing wagon, continue to persevere.

Trust the process, take it day by day, believe God and trust in Him. Persevere and win the race of life! You deserve to experience your best life! A life intended for you to live freely- free of all the things that keep you down. Be kind to yourself, take care of yourself, believe in yourself and your God-given strengths. You have a power and you do not even realize its magnitude.

God's timing is perfect. He will work with you if you allow Him to. He will not force His will upon His children. I am sharing my life story because it is the right time. This is the right time for me as this is where I am in my life's journey. I am empowered and humbled to share my experience in hopes to convey hope and the love of God as I have received it. I feel a sense of responsibility, mostly when I speak to individuals who say they are desperate and have no hope. I am not keeping this blessing to myself- I need to share it. The Lord's message is one of hope and love. Humanity needs love. There is so much hurt and despair. People are searching for God and love in all the wrong places. They will continue to do this if we, the people of the Lord, do not stand up and share the good news. The good news is that there is a God who cares and wants a relationship with them. We cannot see change if we do not accept change.

I have struggled with the decision to share the story of my life for many reasons. One of those reasons is one you may be familiar with, becoming vulnerable with the world. The image of being a strong woman has been important to me, and while growing up, I felt strong because I endured so much and did not ask for help. The reality is being strong and vulnerable are synonymous with each other. It is my life experiences that have taught me that I am the strongest in my weakest moments. *"Our strength is perfected through weakness"* (2 Corinthians 12:9 ESV).

If you have suffered trauma, know that in our most vulnerable moments, it is when we are indeed the strongest. Therefore, seeking counseling, professional support, such as pastoral counseling or professional therapy, is perhaps the best decision you can make for yourself. Getting vulnerable with the right people sets us on a path of victory and healing. It has been a long, long process for me, and it took me a very long time to get here. But that is ok, it is my journey and my healing, and that is precisely how you should feel about your own journey. Do not rush it for God is working with us, and for us, not against us. Nothing is new under the sun; the Lord knows what we are going through. He hears our cry, and He cares.

But He said to me, "My grace is sufficient for you, for my power is made perfect in weakness. Therefore, I will boast all the more gladly of my weaknesses, so that the power of Christ may rest upon me."

2 Corinthians 2:19 (ESV)

Chapter 20

Celebrate Your Life!

Anyone who knows me knows that I celebrate my birthday as if I was one year old again. I celebrate my life because I value my life. You see, today, I love my life. But there was a time in my life when I thought I was worthless, and my life was meaningless. There was so much pain and sorrow. This, of course, was before Jesus came into my life and changed it. I also want to share that just because you come to accept Jesus as your Lord and Savior does not mean you will not feel the pain that has been brewing in your life. This may take time. I urge you to do what you must do: pray, ask the Holy Spirit to guide you, meditate on the Word, eat well, sleep well, take your vitamins, seek someone you trust, or a helping professional. The Word of God has the power to heal you. However, you must do your part. Meet God halfway. It does not mean God cannot heal you on the spot. It means He created you in His image. He knows you have the power to have success in everything you do because He created you. Give yourself a chance.

Honor the things that make you who you are, celebrate yourself. Folks have shared with me how difficult it has been for them to live their lives. Cultural traditions and belief systems have hindered their ability or desire to live the life they want to live. Even Jesus said, *"...And why do you break the commandment of God for your tradition?"* (Matthew 15:3 ESV).

God intended for us to live an abundant life. Our lives are a gift from God. We were born to manifest His glory as we are His most incredible creation. Therefore, I choose to live my life to the fullest. If you have been wronged or have done things in life that you are not proud of, ask God for forgiveness, ask for forgiveness of those you wronged, and forgive yourself. If the people you hurt are not around, write a letter and mail it (even if you do not have an address), burn it, or do some ritual representing closure for you, but you must forgive. It is essential for your healing; it is beneficial for you; forgiveness is a gift; you deserve to be happy and live a healthy life. Now, go live a full life. Do what makes you happy, do good, and live according to God's will (1 Thessalonians 5:16-18 ESV).

"The thief comes only to steal and kill and destroy. I have come that they may have life and have it to the full."

John 10:10 (NIV)

Chapter 21
The Perfect Daughter

How many of tried or are still trying to be the perfect daughter? I did, time and time again I tried to be the perfect little girl for my mother and father. Although they did not intentionally place that burden on me, parents tend to make their children feel like they must be perfect. But no one is perfect. The only time we are perfect is through Jesus. Our Father God sees us through Him. Unintentionally, I also placed those expectations onto my children. When I realized it, I started to ask for forgiveness and began to rectify the situation. No wonder I acted as if God was mad at me. Somewhere along my life's journey, I must have started to believe that God was an angry Father. There are two different facts to consider. One, yes, the bible specifies *"fear of the Lord"* (Proverbs 9:10 NIV). Which will imply that we must fear God. But not in the way fear is used, like in scary movies. But more out of respect for God. I call it "the fearful gospel." However, we are not supposed to bring souls to Christ through fear.

I am so happy I developed this thirst for the truth, God made me this way. I picked up the bible and studied it myself. And God showed up. He is real in my life. Just like I am writing and sharing with you today. I speak with God.

No one is lying to me anymore about God or what He expects of me. Please wake up, my beautiful people. You have the power too; read the bible and ask God to reveal himself to you. Do not just rely on pastors, leaders, or other people to explain God to you. Meet Him for yourself. Get to know your Father. He wants a relationship with you. He loves you! Secondly, yes, God is a God of love and discipline. But the way God disciplines is with love. He gave us free will to do what we want to do and be open to making our own decisions. If that is not love, then what is?

And yes, He is the perfect example of how we should be parenting our children. The Lord says, "here are my commandments" (Exodus 20 NIV). He expects us to follow them. If we do not, we will suffer consequences. But is this God being mad at us? Or this is God saying, I gave you some specific guidelines and life's rules to follow; what did you do? We serve a God of integrity; He does not go back on His Word. He allows us to make the decisions, but it is only fair that we also are responsible and accountable human beings and that we face our own consequences. Yes! That is our God. *We serve an awesome God!* It is interesting to me how we are quick to blame Him for everything, but we do not follow His will for our lives.

> *"For the Lord Most High is to be feared [and worshipped with awe-inspired reverence and obedience- He is a great King over all the earth"*
>
> Psalm 47:2 (AMP)

Chapter 22
What is God's Will for You?

You may be someone I used to be, and I asked this very same question. One of the same questions I still receive from many women. What is God's will for my life? While growing up, I was feeling lost- what is my purpose? Why am I here? I was searching for my reason to be. It seemed unreal to me; this is it? Deep down inside, I knew we are all born with a purpose. I would say to the Lord, "show me, Father God." And He did. The Word of God shows us that confusion is not of the Lord. As I got closer to God, things became more evident. My healing journey began, and I was able to see the light—the guiding light on the path to my reason for being in this world. I am light. And so are you, my friend. God wants to bring light to a world that is so dark. He wants to bring joy where there is sorrow and restore all that has been broken. If you feel lost and broken, come to the light, and your path to restoration, His name is Jesus. He died for you and me so that we can be saved and, in the meantime, find our way through this journey called life.

"Rejoice always, pray continually, give thanks in all circumstances; for this is the will of God for you in Christ Jesus" (1 Thessalonians 5:16-18 NIV).

What I love most about this bible verse in Thessalonians is that it is simple. Rejoice, pray, and give thanks. Yet how many of us are rejoicing in everything, praying continually, and giving thanks for everything? Not many of us, I can tell you that much. If we only knew *"that God [who is deeply concerned about us] causes all things to work together [as a plan] for good for those who love God, to those who are called according to His plan and purpose"* (Romans 8:28 AMP). We would think and behave differently.

I remember the times when things did not go as planned. I used to panic! Now, my response is, "ok Lord, I do not know what you are doing, or what you have saved me from, or where you are leading me to, but I can rest assure you are in control of all things; you are my Father and know what is best for me, your plans for me are not for harm, I can trust you will see all of it through, and you will be by my side." Hallelujah! Yes! He has done this for me time and time again. That is who our Father is, a loving and caring God, who cares about what happens to us.

How do I know? I did not always have joy, pray continually, or gave thanks. But I did complain. Please understand, complaining steals your happiness and stops you from seeing the blessings right in front of you. I was looking for happiness in all the wrong places. I was ungrateful; I spent my time complaining about what I did not have, instead of being thankful for what I did have. I bought my first house in my early twenties, yet I found a reason to complain.

As I got closer to God and His will for my life, things started to fall into place. Even though I struggle with obedience, I pray about any decisions I must make. Let me give you a word of advice if you allow me- obey God. He knows better and it will save you from a lot of heartaches. My approach was to argue with God instead of obeying Him. I cannot stress this enough- *He knows better.* Years later, I can appreciate how God has placed so many things into my life to bring me to this very moment. Obeying God is critical if you want to find peace and clarity in your life. So, let me ask you, what are you complaining about and why are you not obeying God?

"Rejoice always and delight in your faith; be unceasing and persistent in prayer; in every situation [no matter what the circumstances] be thankful and continually give thanks to God; for this is the will of God for you in Christ Jesus"

1 Thessalonians 5:16-18 (AMP)

Chapter 23
Standing in His Love

Jesus is my rock, my fortress, in whom I trust. I firmly believe that if it were not for the love of God, I would not be writing this book. I was searching for a reason in all the wrong places. Only when I gave myself entirely to the Lord, I felt like I was home. Writing my story is freeing in so many ways. I see writing my story as a form of healing. Making sense of our life experiences makes us whole again. There is a reason for what has happened in our lives. Sometimes it is in our control, and sometimes it is not. I encourage you to write your story. You do not have to publish it, but if you do, that is another element of healing. Writing our stories helps us see things from many different perspectives. It helps us reflect on our experiences on a deeper level. You can connect with your innermost being and assess your areas of strength and areas in need of improvement.

You will begin to see when you have been right or wrong and you will be able to validate your own experiences and feelings like never before. There were some things I wanted to share and other things I did not. For a moment, I would think, who cares, or that is just for me to know, and then there were times when I knew I was holding myself back. Our healing journey on earth can be continual. Daily experiences are moments for growth and learning. As human beings, we are continually evolving, and we must assess our attitude towards these experiences. When I feel I have overcome one area of life, I realize there is still much work to be done. One of my favorite sayings is "be patient, God is not finished with me yet." According to His Word, this will occur when He comes back to make everything right.

"The Lord is my rock, my fortress and my deliverer; my God is my rock, in whom I take refuge, my shield and the horn of my salvation, my stronghold"

Psalm 18:2 (NIV)

Chapter 24
Whole, Healthy and Complete

Repeat after me, "I am whole, healthy, and complete." I say this to myself at least once a day. It is one of my daily affirmations. I am sure I annoy my daughters all the time, but I want them to understand something. We are who we say we are. Words have power; the Word of God says it, so it must be true. Self-talk is the best kind of therapy.

The very first experience I had with positive self-talk was when I was about 14 years old. I had to learn to say, "I am beautiful." This was far from what I believed about myself, but with all the abuse I endured, I grew up thinking I looked like a "monster." Just like you read it- a monster. My view of myself was distorted. I was not particularly eager to look at myself in the mirror, and I avoided them. I remember thinking, am I pretty? Deep inside, I wanted to be loved. I longed for more attention. I did anything anyone asked me to do because I wanted to be accepted and loved. After all, that was what I learned. Any rejection was like a stab in my heart, I could not bear it. Just like negative self-talk affects us, so does positive self-talk. We are too hard on ourselves; we can quickly recognize others' strengths and not our own. Be kind to yourself, celebrate who you are, celebrate your accomplishments and your failures. They are lessons to be learned. No one is perfect on this earth, and therefore we should not expect ourselves to be perfect.

As I got closer to God and His Word, God showed me that I am whole and complete. He said that my worth is more than precious rubies (Proverbs 3:15 AMP). I have learned that you take care of yourself when you love and value yourself as God does. For example, you are more kind to yourself by eating better and exercising. You may also speak kindlier to yourself. For every negative talk, replace it with God's promises.

Nothing is new under the sun, ladies, and gentlemen. King David would talk to his soul and remind his soul to bless the Lord (Psalm 103 ESV). The Holy Spirit that was deposited in our lives will guide us. Listen to its voice when it speaks. How would you know, you ask? You will.

We all will have difficult times and challenging days. Let's not forget that we still live in a sinful world; daily stressors will challenge us to stay hopeful and prayerful. Christians are not exempt from being sad or having problems. In fact, we are the enemy's perfect target population. To remind us to stay prayerful and talk to ourselves is essential. We are our worst critic, or our number one cheerleader. You need to decide to see yourself and love yourself as God does. On my worst days, I think about what Jesus did for me at the cross. Even more, I think about what He endured for those three years on earth. He was rejected, ridiculed, bullied, betrayed, tortured, and crucified. Nothing I am going through today will amount to the extent to which our Lord suffered. And yet, He remained focused on the mission at hand. And that beautiful mission was to provide us with eternal life. Not only to live happily ever after when that day comes but to live NOW, with the power and authority given to us through his resurrection. We are not alone. He left us the Holy Spirit to help us. Pray to your soul. Remind yourself how loved and worthy you are. Remind yourself there is hope and a beautiful future ahead. We must persevere. Do not give up. Stay the course. Look up! Cheer for your life and keep going. I know I am! Are you?

"Bless the Lord oh my soul, and all that is within me, bless His Holy Name"

Psalm 103 (ESV)

Chapter 25

Prepare for the Battle

We must wake up every day prepared for battle.

On one occasion, a young lady said to me, "now that I have decided to follow Jesus, everything is going wrong in my life. I am having more problems." To which I responded, "of course, you will." The enemy is not bothering anyone that is not a child of the Lord with such force. You see, he knows he is defeated, and his days are numbered. He is fervently trying to take down as many people as he can along with him. We must wake up every day, ready for battle. I read somewhere, "be the kind of woman that when she wakes up, the devil says, oh, oh, she's up."

The Word of God says, put on the armor of the Lord. Our fight is not against flesh and blood; our battle is spiritual. Therefore, we need spiritual warfare (Ephesians 6:11-18 AMP). Get up every day, and decide that today will be a good day, a day of faith and victory; pray and read your bible even before you get out of bed. Use the words of your mouth to encourage and lift others. Be kind to yourself and others. Congregate with brothers and sisters; you are not alone. God has placed individuals in your life to pray over you and assist you.

Prepare for the Battle

The problem is we do not trust or believe. Do not be afraid for the Lord is with us. The enemy cannot be in the same place as God. Do not allow him to deceive you. Believe in God. Take a chance, and walk by faith, not by sight.

All these lessons I learned through personal experience. I did not know how to fight the schemes of the enemy, but now I do. I will not be toyed with anymore. I choose to fight.

> *"Put on the full armor of God, so that you can take your stand against the devil's schemes."*
>
> Ephesians 6:11 (ESV)

Chapter 26

It is All Part of the Process

If you are anything like me, you want to know everything from the beginning. If you are going to do something, you want to see it through from beginning to end. I want to know the who, the what, the how, and the when. I realize, it is ok not to know everything. Today, I do not strive to know everything; there is a responsibility that comes to knowing. Instead, I want to invest my energy in the wisdom I need to have, and I continue to learn to trust God and rely on His knowledge to make sense of my experiences. God knows best.

One of the practices I do when I am feeling like "this is not going to work out" is to revisit the many times God came through for me and the times I overcame situations I thought were impossible to overcome. I encourage you to do the same. Especially when you are feeling down or sad, take out those beautiful letters someone wrote about you. People may call me nuts, but I save the cards people gift to me. Especially the ones which state how I made someone feel or encouraged them in some way. I keep the cards and letters I receive from students thanking me or sharing how they felt empowered to achieve their goals when someone believed in them. We must "toot our own horn," like one of my mentors used to tell me all the time. "Maribel, toot your own horn."

Seriously, you must be your #1 cheerleader. You have enough people in the world rooting against you, and I am not even talking about the adversary, the enemy. I am talking about some people who for whatever reason did not achieve their dreams, and now they rain on everyone else's parade. Sometimes this is unintentional, but other times it is intentional. I cannot tell you how many times I shared a vision, and people looked at me as if I was crazy, instead of believing or providing support. Therefore, if you are a parent, I am asking you to encourage and support your children in their wildest dreams. What's the worst that can happen?

Life is for dreamers! Only when I dreamt, I felt alive. If I would have chosen to focus on the things around me, in this imperfect world, I would fall apart. Sadness and hopelessness would fill me. I refuse to live that way because I believe the Lord created us to live in abundance. Memorize this verse, write it out, and place it somewhere in your home or office where you are forced to see it and read it every day. God has a plan, and it is for your good.

"For I know the plans I have for you," declares the Lord, "plans to prosper you and not to harm you, plans to give you hope and a future"

Jeremiah 29:11 (NIV)

Chapter 27
Chase Your Dreams

What do you dream about? What are your desires? I often get asked how I continue to chase my dreams. I want to live a full life. When I was younger, I would say, I would retire at the age of 35. My ideology was, *I am not waiting to be happy and live my best life!* I am going to do it now while young. And although that may seem farfetched, it kept me going.

We must ask God for revelation. The Word says we were made for so much more. So many people are "stuck." Why? What things must we resolve to move forward? Take an inventory of your life. Sometimes thoughts about our past failures hold us back. I do not want to live like that. It is not healthy. If we "fail" at something, then start again.

Anytime I thought about starting something new, I would immediately think, "well, do you want to try that again?" And just as fast, I would think YES! You never know what you can do until you try—getting stuck in what never happened just fuels negativity and non-productivity. Try this:

1. Assess what happened before.

2. Evaluate the "why's" for wanting to go after your dreams again and start again.

3. Once you have a clear vision of what you want to do, go for it, and give it your all.

4. Do not expect people to always buy into your goals and dreams. If the Lord revealed it to you, it is for you to pursue it.

5. Remember, we are part of God's plan and He will not let you fail.

He will help you see it through. Make amends with past situations, forgive yourself, and start again. Perseverance is the name of the game. Never give up! That is my motto.

"Commit to the Lord whatever you do, and He will establish your plans."

Proverbs 16:3 (NIV)

Chapter 28
Do Not Give Your Power Away

I learned this the hard way. I felt powerless for so many years. I was not able to defend myself from the evildoers in my life. And I was not speaking up about what happened to me. I felt powerless. Jesus said, *"I have given you authority to trample on snakes and scorpions and to overcome all the power of the enemy; nothing will harm you"* (Luke 10:19 NIV). Jesus died and rose again to give us power and authority. Think about the ultimate gift, eternal life. Because of His sacrifice, we have a second chance in life. I have learned that I have the dominion over things on earth, that whatever I bind on earth, shall be bound in Heaven as well (Genesis 1:26-28 NIV; Matthew 18:18 KJV). The Word of God is power. Please do not give it away. I like to read the Word of God and apply it in practical ways. For me, power is the ability to do something. God said we have power, so I walk in power (2 Timothy 1:7 NIV).

Decide to take control of your life today. Make wise decisions. Decide what you will or will not allow in your life. We have the OK from God to walk with this authority. I do not like the words, "I cannot," because you can do all things through Christ. We can because He has given us everything, we need in order to succeed (Philippians 4:13 NIV; 2 Peter 1:3 NIV). How we activate this power is through wise decisions, but when we are in doubt, we must seek first the kingdom of God (Matthew 6:33 NIV). Find a spiritual mentor to help you make sense of things difficult to understand. Read the Word daily. Your life depends on it.

What are some of the lies we believe?

- I am not good enough
- I am not loved
- I am not smart
- I am not worthy
- I cannot do anything right

Those were some of the lies that were instilled in you, but they do not need to remain in you. If you are reading this book it is because you are searching, and you hear God's voice. You are seeking, and He is answering. As imperfect human beings, we are quick to point out that He is not answering our prayers or things are not going our way. But the simple act of picking up this book tells me that you are searching, and He is answering. I was looking for God and thought He was not around. The reality is that He is always around.

We need to walk with the new truth in our lives, not walk like we are defeated souls. That is what the enemy wants us to feel, defeated. I am here to tell you that we are more than conquerors, new creations. The moment you accepted Christ as your Lord and Savior, you adopted a new way of life and thinking. *"Therefore, if anyone is in*

Christ, the new creation has come: The old has gone, the new is here" (2 Corinthians 5:17 NIV).

"I am not good enough," this is what the world has made you believe in hard times. Perhaps you believe that you did not have the best relationship with your parents, or that you did not have a great childhood. None of that means that you are not good enough, for you are *"God's handy work created in Christ Jesus to do good works, which God prepared in advance for us to do"* (Ephesians 2:10 NIV). Remember that He knew you before you were even born. Have faith in God for He knows what He is doing. He created your beautiful soul.

A famous lie the enemy wants us to believe is that we are *not loved*, wanted, accepted, or appreciated. That is the biggest lie yet, we are so loved that God gave *"His one and only son, so that whoever believes in him not perish, but have eternal life"* (John 3:16 NIV). Why would our creator give His only son for us if He did not love us? Why do we even have redemption? The problem is that we have bought into the "love," society, and romantic relationships have taught us.

The enemy does not care about that specifically. He cares about God's love and self-love. Meaning, if he succeeds in making you believe that you are not loved, then he has won over you. How so? Think about it, God is love and we are made in His image. If the enemy succeeds in destroying how you view yourself, then he has succeeded in you not loving God or living a Godly, victorious life. Your image is distorted, which in turn will affect your confidence and trust in God. He knows his days are numbered; he is doing his very best to take down as many people as possible. Brothers and sisters, this is serious. The Gospel of Jesus is about love, because of love you are saved. Do not let the enemy deceive you. Take back the power.

"I am not smart enough," this lie is one that I still battle with. Whenever I embark on a new project, training, or a quiz, I continue to battle this lie. Did I mention I am a professor? Professor or not, this is something I have battled with all my life. This is also something I have shared with my students frequently, "You do not have to be smart to be in college. You need to be smart enough to know what's best for you."

Life learning is the best thing. If you have a spirit of always wanting to learn and grow, that is priceless! You do not need to know everything; you just need to have the desire and determination to achieve it. Do not let the enemy manipulate you into thinking you are not smart enough because this will exhaust you and keep you from the best things in life. You will give up before you even start. Take control. You have the mind of Christ (1 Corinthians 2:16 NIV).

"*I am not worthy."* Feelings of unworthiness were feelings I struggled with for most of my life. A woman who knows her worth is powerful. Feelings of unworthiness leave us feeling insufficient, that we have no value, and undeserving of love or affection. It affects our self-esteem, and we feel powerless. I am here to tell you, that is a lie. We are so valuable to God that He has adopted us into His family of royalty, a chosen generation (1 Peter 2:9 KJV). We are co-heirs with Christ, Jesus! We are the head, not the tail (Deuteronomy 28:13 AMP).

"I cannot do anything right." This is another lie. The Lord says that there is nothing we cannot do, especially if it is aligned with His will for our lives (Philippians 4:13 AMP; Romans 8:28, AMP). He has the last word. We, the children of the Lord, seek guidance, ask for wisdom, and wait patiently while trusting that God's got us. *"He who began the work in us will see it through"* (Philippians 1:6 NIV). But when you think you are not able, remember who is capable and who you belong to. This is why this is a lie, because although we may think we are not able, God is able, and the God we serve "is able to make all grace abound toward you; that you, always having all sufficiency in all things, may abound to every good work."

You see, we are not doing things alone. Our heavenly Father promised us. He will not forsake us. And remember, He is not a man that can lie. He is our God the Almighty, the Omnipotent powerful God. If we are with Him, who is against us? Everything I have done and am is because of God. I have done nothing alone. I am nothing without God. I know that I may fail in my strength, but I know that I will never fail with God. When you think, "I am not capable," always remember you are not alone, and you are more than capable.

"Now to Him who is able to [carry out His purpose and] do superabundantly more than all that we dare ask or think [infinitely beyond our greatest prayers, hopes, or dreams], according to His power that is at work within us"

Ephesians 3:20 (AMP)

Chapter 29
God is Not Mad at You!

Every time I did something wrong or disobeyed God, I thought God was mad at me. I felt I was to blame for what happened to me, and then when it did happen, I blamed myself for not talking about it or mentioning it to anyone. I would punish myself by not going to church. Somehow, I knew that going to church was a good thing. That is one of the ways I tortured myself. I knew I belonged to God and that there was no escaping from what God had in store for me. I thought God was mad at me because I did not want to forgive those who hurt me. I thought that it was not fair, and why should I be the one to forgive when they were the ones who should be asking me for forgiveness.

I thought God was mad at me because I did not want to submit myself to studying the Word, pray for hours on end, or be nice to the people at church who were not so nice to me. Christians hurt people too. Sometimes, this is the worst kind of pain because they are not embodying Christ, but they still get forgiven. Because of my sinful condition, I thought God was mad at me. I was blaming myself for all the wrongdoings done to me. I missed the whole message. Do not let this happen to you. God loves you just as you are! He is our redeemer; He wants to bring healing to our hearts and souls.

The devil wants us to feel guilt, shame, and doubt because he is defeated. He wants us to feel powerless, because then, God does not get glorified. The whole message is that we are not perfect. Therefore, it is good for our souls to seek the Lord, our Creator, the one who knows how to fix us and redeem us. Halleluiah! I LOVE our GOD! He already knows there is nothing you need to say or do to earn His love. It is done! You are loved; you were bought by His precious blood for His glory.

Think about when you create something, you are so proud that you want to show it off. Well, God wants to show you off. Look at my creation; they are not perfect, but they are mine, and I love them with eternal love. If only they knew. I can almost hear God say this, but I can also feel him weeping for His children and asking himself, what are they thinking? What are they doing? Why do they not believe in me? How can I reach them and tell them how much I love and want them to be saved? Do not get it twisted. He will correct us where we need to be corrected, but He loves us and will do this in love. How many times did I use love in this section? Many times. It is intentional. Someone reading this needs to know this, *you are loved!* That is the best message you can ever receive. Do not live in bondage anymore; God hurts because you hurt. Jesus died to set us free. Free from all the sin of this world.

"The Lord is gracious and full of compassion, slow to anger and abounding in lovingkindness."

Psalm 145:8 (AMP)

Chapter 30

Spring Cleaning, Lessons Learned

The lessons learned are too many to count. I want to share a few. One of the most important lessons I have learned is that nothing is as it seems. Therefore, we should never assume anything. Do not judge the book by its cover because it is almost always deceiving. My father used to tell me, "Maribel try things out for yourself, everyone is different, and your likes and dislikes are different from others." People are quick to give you their opinion about things. It is okay to hear them out but learn to make your own decisions. It is wise to seek counsel. Those are two different things. Beliefs usually come with personal biases and pre-conceived notions. Wisdom usually comes from someone who has had some experience, may be considered an expert on the subject, and does not lose or gain anything from sharing. When you need wisdom from someone, please do your research and make sure it is the right person to talk to about the specific situation you are asking questions about.

Too often, we share things with people regardless of their expertise or knowledge. We share without completely processing, "is this the right person to share this with?" Sometimes we say things to the wrong person, and they lead us in the wrong direction. I have learned that people speak out of their own condition; The Word of God reminds us, "*A good man brings good things out of the good stored up in his heart, and an evil man brings evil things out of the evil stored up in his heart. For the mouth speaks what the heart is full of*" (Luke 6:45 NIV). Therefore, they may feel what happened to them will happen to you. If they have been hurt, they will speak out of pain if it has not been healed. Before communicating with anyone or asking for advice, seek out God for He will not lead you astray. He will answer your prayer and will place the right people in your life to guide you through the process. Ask Him to reveal those individuals to you.

Another important lesson; forgive to be forgiven. One of the things that holds us back is unforgiveness. For the longest time, I felt I had forgiven all who had hurt me. I was wrong. Every time I would soul-search, I would notice there was one more person or situation to forgive. Just like when you do spring cleaning every year, you must do the same with your heart. Remove all that is harmful and unpleasing to God. Be honest with yourself; write down the things you know are affecting you negatively. These may include relationships, foods you are consuming, or things you are watching or listening to. Human beings are sensitive; things affect us more than we know.

Walk around your house and remove everything that hinders your life. Think about the things that make you sad, frustrated, or angry. My home is my safe haven.

When I look at the rooms in my house, I love what I see. They bring me joy. If something in my home does not bring me joy, I change it. Why would you keep something in your home that does not bring you joy? I have an area of the house where I keep the grandchildren's toys. For some, this may be a mess. For me, it brings me happiness when I see them. I can picture their little faces light up with their toys. My oldest grandson says, "*Eela, you love me so much, this is my space.*" When he sees this area, he knows he is loved, and he belongs here.

Do not become attached to material things on this earth. Cherish and treasure what matters most. We are just passing through. This is not our home. (Hebrews 13:14 ESV).

All Scripture is breathed out by God and profitable for teaching, for reproof, for correction, and for training in righteousness, that the man of God may be competent, equipped for every good work.

2 Timothy 3:16-17 (ESV)

Chapter 31

Live the Life God Intended for You

I hope that when you read this book, you are inspired to live the life that God intended for you to live. I hope you find it in your heart to forgive yourself and stop punishing yourself for whatever situations were brought into your life. You are forgiven. We often walk in shame because we think we did something wrong and are forever blaming ourselves. On top of that, we believe God is also making a list and checking twice. He is not Santa Clause. The Word says, *"He casts all our sins into the depths of the sea"* (Micah 7:19 ESV). Thank God, hallelujah! The Lord knows all my sins. For we have *"all fallen short of the glory of God"* (Romans 3:23 ESV).

I hope that if you do not know God, by reading this book, you meet with your Heavenly Father and accept Him as your Lord and savior. But if you have met Him and have strayed away, I hope that you fall in love with God all over again and give him another chance. His Word says, *"If you remain in me and my words remain in you, ask whatever you wish, and it will be done for you"* (John 15:7 NIV). God loves you so much that He wants to restore your life. It does not matter what has happened in the past; what matters is the decision you make from here on out. Choose to continue to live your best life and honor Him in all you do. For when you honor yourself, you honor God. How might you start honoring yourself today?

Do not harbor any secrets, secrets have power. When you keep things a secret, they hurt. Sometimes more than you think. The secrets that I am referring to are the secrets that bring you shame, guilt, and doubt. The shameful secrets are usually brought upon you with and without your consent. Many families have secrets, and if you have not figured out by now, these secrets destroy families. Do not allow this to happen in your life. The devil wants to destroy families because this way he destroys a society of hope. Be sure to schedule a family meeting and do a family health checkup. Do not leave any open doors or windows. The enemy will do as he pleases when we allow him. The Word says, *"Submit yourselves, then, to God. Resist the devil, and he will flee from you"* (James 4:7 NIV). Resist doing wrong and do what is right. For example, if someone wrongs you, forgive fast. Do not leave any room for the enemy to torment you. The devil despises love and unity because God is love and unity. Where there is love, there is God. The enemy does not like this. Take back the control, remember God said we have "the power of self-control," take it back from the enemy and restore your lives. That is the authority Jesus talks about. Do not walk as if you are defeated because we are not defeated.

There were times in my life when I made great strides, and then there were times that I was stuck. In my search for answers and was not progressing, I would ask God, "what am I doing wrong, Lord? Why do I not advance?" The Lord made it clear to me that I was stuck because I had not forgiven. I would say, "Lord, I forgave him, and all the people who hurt me!" God would show me that I did not. For some, forgiveness is hard to do. However, it is the greatest reward. Before you know it, you are stuck again, and you do not know why. Look deep into your soul and your actions. They will show you if you have forgiven those who wronged you.

I realized I had forgiven my parents, because I am able to have a relationship with them without any animosity. I know I forgave my uncle because I do not have any ill feelings towards him. My hopes and prayers are that he has been saved. I never had the chance to tell him that I forgave him because I never saw him again. We think that he has passed. We believe that he developed a fatal illness and did not last, but no one knows for sure.

When I learned about his childhood and upbringing, my heart was full of sadness for him. I guess he was not preached the gospel or perhaps, he rejected it. I do not know because I never had this discussion with him, and I wish I could have.

Christians, we can help many people if we do our part. I wondered if anyone ever preached the gospel to my uncle. He grew up alone in the streets for the most part. If it was not because of my mom, who took him in, where would he have been? My mother has the biggest heart. Those who know her know that she would take the clothes from her back to give to someone in need.

My uncle had a home and food because of my mom. I wish I would have had the opportunity to look him in the eye and tell him that I forgave him. I wish we would have had the opportunity to restore our lives as uncle and niece. If I could tell him anything, it would be "I love you, and I forgive you. I am sorry for what others did to you." I know he was hurt because, as Joyce Meyers says, "hurt people hurt people." This is true.

You, who are reading this, know that you are still hurt if you do not forgive, and your framework is pain. It is commonly known; you will hurt those around you because you are hurt. Those around you will pay for what others did to you, without fault.

Profoundly reflect on this topic and be true to yourself. Reflect on your actions and weed out anything that is not pleasing to God. Once you reflect on your actions, ask yourself, who do I still need to forgive? Why do I act this way with this person? Why do I not like this individual? Do they trigger something in me? Do they remind me of someone who hurt me? Explore, are you angry? What are you angry about? Anger is a symptom of pain.

In the following chapter, you will see the letter I wrote of forgiveness to myself, and perhaps it can help you to start your own.

Chapter 32

I Forgive You

Mari, it is time to let go of the guilt, the shame, and all the pain that is still hurting you. What your uncle did to you is not your doing; you did not do anything wrong. You were just a little girl who was afraid and terrified. For years you have felt guilt, shame, and feelings of unworthiness, for something you did not do.

Mari, I forgive you for not saying anything. I forgive you because you did not know what to do or where to go. You felt alone.

I forgive you for hurting yourself and trying to end your precious life. A life that was given to you to live in abundance. You were created with a purpose. You were not an accident.

Mari, I forgive you for not protecting your sisters. You tried. You were just a little girl. You did not deserve this pain. He did this to you. He instilled this in you. He lied to you. He manipulated you and frightened you. He abused you.

Beautiful Mari, I forgive you for being hard on yourself and setting unreachable goals and expectations that were totally out of your control.

Mari, I forgive you for not protecting your children from the evil in this world. You did your best, to the best of your abilities.

Maribel, the Lord Jesus loves you, and He died for your sins. "There is no condemnation to those who love the Lord" (Romans 1:17 KJV). Shame and guilt do not belong to you. They died at the cross when love was born.

Maribel, I forgive you, and I love you more than words can say. Do not allow the enemy to plague you with lies; lies are meant to destroy you because you belong to God. You are beautiful, strong, fearfully, and wonderfully made in God's image.

The Lord, your God, has given you a spirit of love, power, and a sound mind (2 Timothy 1:7 KJV). He has equipped you to face head-on all obstacles that come your way. You are prepared and filled with the Holy Spirit to conquer all.

You *"can do all things through Christ who strengthens you"* (Philippians 4:13 KJV).

Love yourself, I do, and I am so very proud of you. Be free.

Maribel

Now, I am going to ask you to write, perhaps, one of the most challenging letters you will ever write, and embark on a journey of love, freedom, and deliverance. I ask you to place your name in the blank space and say, _____ I forgive you, and start today. Forgive yourself. God already did. He is not mad at you. In fact, He loves you.

This may take you to a place in your memory where you do not want to go to. But if you want healing in your life, if you want the pain to stop, it is a step you MUST take towards your journey of love and freedom.

You are not alone…

"When you pass through the waters, I will be with you; and through the rivers, they shall not overwhelm you; when you walk through fire you shall not be burned, and the flame shall not consume you."

Isaiah 43:2 (ESV)

Chapter 33
God Loves You and I Do Too!

Yes! As simple as that, God loves you and I do too! I am screaming from the top of my lungs! Today, I am proud of the woman I am. You would not recognize me from twenty years ago. I would often ask God, *"How can you love people who hurt people? Why do you want me to love her? I do not like her."* I would ask God, *"please give me the love He has for everyone."* A Spanish song sang in churches called, "Te pido la paz" translates as, "I ask for peace." The beginning of the song says, "ayúdame a mirar con tus ojos, ayúdame a sentir con el corazón," (help me to see with your eyes, help me to feel with your heart). And it goes on to say, I do not want to live with this insensitive heart. There is need on this earth. Then it goes on to ask for peace. You have no idea how I sang this song. As my angry self, I would look at people in the church, which I knew would talk about me. I would sing, *"help me to see with your eyes and help me to feel with your heart,"* because at this very moment, Father, I do not want to look at her or love him. But I kept going, and I reminded myself not to grow weary of doing right. The Word states, *"Let us not become weary in doing good, for at the proper time we will reap a harvest if we do not give up"* (Galatians 6:9 NIV).

Although it may still be challenging at times, it is essential to demonstrate love to those who may seem hard to love. This does not come from me; this comes from my heavenly Father, who has poured out grace into my life and filled it with love. I do not like what a lot of people do, but I can honestly say I love them with the love of Christ. I may not agree with some of their actions, but I know that if God does not give up on them, neither should I. He did not give up on me; why should I give up on them? The Word of God is straightforward. If you judge, you will be judged. With the same measure you measure, you will be measured. Wake up folks, God is real, and He is a righteous God. He will not be mocked, *"Do not be deceived: God cannot be mocked. A man reaps what he sows"* (Galatians 6:7 NIV).

The Lord, our God, our Heavenly Father loves you! And He is calling you back! He is asking for you to come home. How beautiful is that? Think about it, if you are a mother or a father reading this book here today, this one is for you. God loves you, and you especially know the love of a parent and the anguish a parent feels when their child is lost or has gone towards a path of destruction. You would do anything to save your child and have them back home.

For anyone in pain, feeling that you have let God down, God is not mad at you. God is hurting for you, and He is also hurting for the earth. He wants us to turn from our evil ways and come home. For me, it took me a long time before realizing how much God loves me.

I am here to tell you; I have been entrusted with this mission; He knows what you are going through. He is the only one that knows what resides in our hearts. He knows we want to do good and deep down inside we want to live a life worthy of appreciation of the gift of salvation. If you have been struggling with accepting the love of Christ, let me help you. Go into a quiet place and speak to God from your heart. Just as you are, He is waiting at the door. He is waiting for you. He has been there all along. It is us who separate from the love of God- not Him. He wants to restore your life. He wants you to live an abundant life, just as He intended it for all. The Lord wants you to live a life of purpose and love. Remember, He made you in His image and has equipped you to carry on until the day He returns to earth.

God's not mad at you. *He loves you!*

One way the LORD has healed me through His Word, where I found love and redemption by meditating on His Word, was writing down scriptures and studying what the Lord was saying to me. Journaling is healing. If writing is not your preference, then journal with pictures, drawings, or music.

There are different ways we make sense of what we experience in our lives. The important thing is to ask God for guidance through the process. He wants a relationship with you. He wants to bring you peace. It will change your life!

The following reflection questions will get you started on your healing journey.

"Blessed is the one who does not walk in step with the wicked or stand in the way that sinners take or sit in the company of mockers, but whose delight is in the law of the Lord, and who meditates on his law day and night. That person is like a tree planted by streams of water, which yields its fruit in season and whose leaf does not wither—whatever they do prospers."

Psalm 1:1-3 (NIV)

Reflections

Reflections

Chapter 1

Reflection: Have you ever wondered is there a God?

Chapter 2

Reflection: What do you need healing from?

Chapter 3

Reflection: What are the things you need to do to dismantle the lies brought into your life?

Chapter 4

Reflection: What bullies are you fighting off daily?

Chapter 5

Reflection: What area of your life needs God's intervention?

Chapter 6

Reflection: What are you grateful for?

Chapter 7

Reflection: What are you hoping for?

Chapter 8

Reflection: You are who God says you are, say these affirmations daily and do not stop until you believe them! Reflect on these daily affirmations? What other affirmations would you adopt?

- *I am loved*
- *I am forgiven*
- *I am worthy*
- *I am chosen*
- *I am redeemed*
- *I am set apart for greatness*
- *I am royal priesthood*
- *I am beautifully and wonderfully made*
- *I belong to God*

Chapter 9

Reflection: Take a moment to write down the ways in which God has saved you.

Chapter 10

Reflection: Write out the ways God blesses you.

Chapter 11

Reflection: Who inspires you? Why?

Chapter 12

Reflection: What are you asking God for?

Chapter 13

Reflection: Have you ever struggled with identity issues? How did you resolve?

Chapter 14

Reflection: Why is it hard for you to trust God?

Chapter 15

Reflection: What are your beliefs about God?

Chapter 16

Reflection: Who or what is stealing your joy?

Chapter 17

Reflection: Who do you feel responsible for? And why? Who do you need to forgive or ask forgiveness from?

Chapter 18

Reflection: Can you think of a time when God showed

up in your life? Let us go deeper…

Chapter 19

Reflection: Stay focused, it is time to prioritize… list the things, that may be keeping you apart from God and let us put everything in its place.

Chapter 20

Reflection: Celebrate your life! List the things you are proud of…

1.

2.

3.

4.

5.

Chapter 21

Reflection: Read Psalm 47:2 (NIV) What is God saying to you?

Chapter 22

Reflection: What is God's will for your life? (1 Thessalonians 5:16-18 AMP)

Chapter 23

Reflection: What demands have been placed on you?

Chapter 24

Reflection: Repeat after me, "I am whole, healthy, and complete." Now, believe…

Chapter 25

Reflection: The battle; what must you do to prepare for battle? Ephesians 6: 10-18 (AMP)

Chapter 26

Reflection: What do you believe? What battles are you fighting?

Chapter 27

Reflection: What were your dreams growing up? Did you achieve them? What stopped you?

Chapter 28

Reflection: What negative self-talks must you replace with God's promises?

Chapter 29

Reflection: Meditate and memorize this verse:

"For I know the plans I have for you," declares the Lord, "plans to prosper you and not to harm you, plans to give you hope and a future" (Jeremiah 29:11 NIV).

Chapter 30

Reflection: What lessons have you learned in your lifetime?

Chapter 31

Reflection: Who do you need to forgive? Is it yourself?

Chapter 32

Reflection: Write your letter of forgiveness. You will be discouraged by many reasons, and excuses not to write this letter; But I want to encourage you to be courageous and write it, and once you write the letter, read it out loud as many times as you need to. Jesus died for you and me; God forgave us. Now, we must forgive.

Chapter 33

Reflection: God loves you! Do you believe? Reflect on the many ways you see God's love demonstrated in your life.

Reference

Pichere, P., & Cadiat, A.-C. (2015)

> *Maslow's hierarchy of needs.*
>
> Lemaitre.

About the Author

Dr. Maribel López, is an Inspirational Speaker, Author, Professor, and an Ordained Minister, born in the beautiful island of Puerto Rico. She is a wife, mother, and proud grandmother, Lover of Jesus and life! Her purpose is to empower and help individuals heal from the lies plagued and imprinted by childhood sexual abuse and rape. *She desires for people to be free of shame, guilt, condemnation and self-destruction as these were the challenges she had to overcome.* Dr. López teaches, preaches, and ministers locally and internationally. Together with her husband founded Restored Ministries in Illinois and the Dr. Maribel Lopez Scholarship Foundation. Their desire is to see lives restored through the power of love, the study of the Word of God, and biblical teachings.

Other Publications:

Eternally Grateful Journal-Eternamente Agradecida (Diario)

Eternally Grateful-Eternamente Agradecida (2017), is a journal written both in English and Spanish, created with the purpose to help women find healing through the art of journaling the Word of God. Maribel found healing through journaling the Word of God, writing her inner thoughts, and feelings. It is her hope that you may find healing just as she did.

Dr. López Quote of the Week, (Spanish and English)

Dr. López' Quote of the Week Book (also available in Spanish) was inspired by students, and it is for students of all ages. The proceeds from the Dr. López' Quote of the Week book assist students achieve their academic goals through The Dr. Maribel López Scholarship Foundation.

For more information visit:
www.dloscholarshipfoundation.com.

Thank you for your support!

You can purchase both publications at amazon.com

Authors Note

"Thank you for your desire in my ministry and life! God bless you today and always! Together let's make a difference in the lives of individuals who otherwise feel hopeless and powerless."

Join Dr. López on her mission to bring hope and encouragement to lives through the work of God now, here on earth!

-Dr. López

Invite Dr. Maribel López

to your next event!

www.drmaribellopez.com

maribel@drmaribellopez.com

Facebook: https://www.facebook.com/maribelmpkb

Instagram: @drlopez_maribel

Twitter: @drlopez_maribel

www.ingramcontent.com/pod-product-compliance
Lightning Source LLC
Chambersburg PA
CBHW071227090426
42736CB00014B/3003